FRANK LLOYD WRIGHT'S HANNA HOUSE

The Clients' Report

Special thanks go to the San Mateo and the Times Mirror Foundations
whose generous grants helped make possible the publication of this book.

FRANK LLOYD WRIGHT'S HANNA HOUSE

The Clients' Report

Paul R. and Jean S. Hanna

The Architectural History Foundation, New York
The MIT Press, Cambridge, Massachusetts, and London, England

Designed by Paul Grotz

Library of Congress Cataloging in Publication Data
Hanna, Paul Robert, 1902-
    Frank Lloyd Wright's Hanna House.
    (Architectural History Foundation/MIT Press
series ; v. 5)
    Bibliography
    1. Paul R. Hanna House (Stanford, Calif.)
2. Wright, Frank Lloyd, 1867-1959.   3. Usonian houses
—California—Stanford.   4. Hanna, Paul Robert,
1902-   —Homes.   I. Hanna, Jean Shuman.
II. Title.   III. Series.
NA7238.S8H36   728.3'73'0924   81-8374
ISBN 0-262-08109-1   AACR2

Note: The blueprints for Hanna-Honeycomb were labeled "Hanna House" by
Frank Lloyd Wright. Although he referred to the plan as his
"honeycomb" experiment in speaking and writing, he did not combine
the owners' name and the honeybees' contribution on any drawing.

Richard Lyman, President of Stanford University, joined the two
parts of the official name—Hanna-Honeycomb House—in 1972,
when he created the Board of Governors to manage the property.
Since that time the university has consistently joined the name of the
client and the name given by the architect to this first hexagonal
module residence.

For Emily-Jean, John, and Robert

ACKNOWLEDGMENTS

We are grateful to all the many individuals, groups, and institutions that contributed during the past half-century to the life of the Hanna House. Here we wish to record a special debt to those whose valuable contributions are not acknowledged in our text:

Assisting Mr. Wright in designing and supervising our house were: Olgivanna Lloyd Wright, William Wesley Peters, L. Cornelia Brierly, John Howe, John Hill, Aaron Green, Kenneth Lockhart, Tony Puttnam, Eldridge Spencer, Eugene Masselink, Bruce Brooks Pfeiffer, and William Schwarz.

Administrators at Stanford University who sustained us in our enterprise: Presidents Ray Lyman Wilbur, J. E. Wallace Sterling, and Richard Lyman; Vice President Kenneth Cuthbertson; General Secretaries Paul H. Davis and Daryl H. Pearson; Deans John W. Dodds, I. James Quillen, and Virgil Whitaker; Director of Planning M. Harry Sanders, Jr.; Staff Counsel Iris Brest; Chairman of the Board of Trustees, Paul Edwards.

The craftsmen, technicians, and suppliers who shaped the raw materials according to the blueprints of our dwelling.

The Nissan Motor Corporation in U.S.A. who generously endowed, with a half-million-dollar gift to Stanford, "the management, maintenance, and improvement" of the Hanna House; and Mr. William Powell whose gift supplemented the Nissan endowment fund.

The Hoover Institution, whose accommodations, equipment and supplies facilitated our task.

Those who encouraged and advised us in preserving our archives on the Hanna House: Glenn Campbell, Director of the Hoover Institution; Charles Palm, Deputy Archivist at the Hoover Institution; and Roxanne Nilan, Archivist of Stanford University.

The editors of this text: Henry-Russell Hitchcock, Edgar Kaufmann, jr., and Victoria Newhouse.

The friends who read early drafts of some chapters of this manuscript and encouraged us to publish: Reid R. Briggs, H. Allen Brooks, Mitsuya Goto, Ben Raeburn, Harry M. Sanders, Jr., and Paul V. Turner.

Patricia E. Preston, for three years of effective and devoted labor in organizing and inventorying our archives and processing our manuscript.

We are indebted to the many amateur and professional photographers who have composed images of the house through their viewfinders. We are especially grateful for the beautiful color photographs of our friend, Ezra Stoller, who spent several days with us studying and photographing our home. He has captured the essence of Mr. Wright's philosophy of organic architecture.

CONTENTS

Terrace off north end of living room

View of house from Frenchman's Road

10

Brick-faced retaining wall and steps

Frank Lloyd Wright's original rendering of the Hanna House, 1936

INTRODUCTION

Few of Frank Lloyd Wright's clients have published in detail their experiences with him and with the houses he designed for them. Most of those who have written about Mr. Wright's buildings have been architectural historians or journalists, who are usually dependent on secondary sources. We have a different approach.

From 1930, when we first contemplated the possibility of having Mr. Wright design a house for us, we saved almost every item that had any bearing on our association with him or our residence. We have over fifty ring binders, filling over eight feet of shelf space, in which we have organized chronologically our exchange of letters, telegrams, and notes of telephone calls. We have about one hundred drawings and blueprints prepared by Mr. Wright and his associated architects. We have more than two hundred black-and-white or color photographs by professionals.* We took several hundred photographs ourselves during the various phases of construction.

Our archives contain legal documents, contracts, and specifications; payrolls, bills, and receipts; correspondence with other architects, with banks, and with the administration of Stanford University; hundreds of letters requesting visiting privileges and hundreds more thanking us for the visits. We have preserved magazine and newspaper stories about our house and assembled books in which some aspect of the house is presented.

With these archives before us, we have refreshed and corrected our memories of what, when, how, and why we planned, built, and lived in a house Frank Lloyd Wright designed. We have presented the story as we believe it happened—a balance of frustration and satisfaction on the part of all of us who played a role.

We intend to let the documents themselves present the quality of our relationships with Mr. Wright, with the administration of Stanford University, and with the many people who have been involved in our endeavor. Particularly, we believe that reading correspondence, telegrams, and reported conversations with Mr. Wright permits a proper evaluation of the man, his philosophy, and his work.

Our Wright archives, covering a period from 1930 to 1980, are deposited in the Stanford University Library. Microfilms of the entire collection are available through the Architectural History Foundation.

People continue to ask to visit the house. Volunteers from The Committee for Art of the Stanford Museum escort small parties through the Hanna House by appointment on certain days of the month. Inquiries may be made through the office of Educational Services at the Stanford Museum.

* Morley Baer, Esther Born, John Engstead, Yukio Futagawa, Leo Holub, Ezra Stoller, the Palo Alto Times, Stanford News and Publications Service, Sunset Magazine, and others.

13

Aerial view of the Hanna House, 1952

CHAPTER ONE

A Home of Our Own

THERE was a *raison d'être* for our consuming interest in house building. As ministers' children, both of us had grown up in Minnesota in a succession of parsonages provided by the congregations our fathers were serving. Most of our experiences as children growing up in these parsonages were positive. It was taken for granted that one listened to good music, read stimulating books and magazines, engaged in serious conversations, entertained guests from places near and far, and generally enjoyed family life. But every three to five years a minister was reassigned to a different parish. We were not free to remake a parsonage building to suit our particular preferences and needs. Such restrictions developed in both of us a desire to design and build a house to meet our own life-styles. And, most passionately, each of us longed to own a home and live in it permanently.

We met in college as freshmen and fell in love. During the four years of courtship and two years of engagement, we dreamed about a home of our own. From the time we were married in 1926, we kept folders containing architectural ideas. At first we were able to visualize only one room at a time. Gradually we began to think in terms of the whole house. We discovered the Bauhaus movement and read everything we could find on German architecture. Mostly we were confused. We could not formulate or express a basic philosophy of architecture.

We were teaching at Columbia University when, in 1930, we came upon newspaper reports of the Kahn Lectures by Frank Lloyd Wright at Princeton. We secured the published volume of lectures and sat up all night reading and rereading *Modern Architecture* aloud to each other. Certain adages in that volume expressed for us a philosophy of home and of living that moved us deeply:

Principle is the safe precedent.

The working of a principle is the only safe tradition.

An organic form grows its structure out of conditions as a plant grows out of soil. Both unfold similarly from within.

Form is organic only when it is natural to materials and natural to function.

An inner-life principle is a gift to every seed. An inner-life is also necessary for every idea of a good building.

Simplicity and style are both consequences, never causes.

Specific purpose is the qualifying aim of all creation.

From the ground up is good sense for building. Beware of from the top down.

Form is made by function but qualified by use. Therefore, form changes with changing conditions. The last analysis is never made.

All forms stand prophetic, beautiful, and forever in so far as they were in themselves truth embodied. They become ugly and useless only when forced to seem and be what they are not and cannot be.

Creation never imitates. Creation assimilates.

By morning we were inspired to write a fan letter to Mr. Wright thanking him for his statement which expressed concepts we had sensed but had never been able to articulate.

Much to our delight, Mr. Wright responded and invited us to visit him in his Taliesin home in Spring Green, Wisconsin. In the summer of 1931 we drove to visit our families in Minnesota and routed ourselves through Wisconsin, hoping that Mr. Wright would not have forgotten his generous invitation.

The Wrights and their extended household welcomed us warmly. We spent twenty-four hours there listening to Mr. Wright. We recall vividly the main thrust of his discussion—four principles of organic architecture: respect for the site (environment), for materials, and for the past, and sensitivity to the aspirations and requirements of clients.

We recall only vaguely that Mr. Wright spoke casually of his hope someday to abandon boxlike, right-angle corners and to design and build with the more flexible hexagonal forms of the bees' honeycomb. We were too inexperienced to comprehend the significant innovation Mr. Wright was conceiving in adapting the cross section of the honeycomb design.

Those hours at Taliesin gave us far more than theory. We were enthralled by the spell of that lovely home. We felt we were fortunate to get to know Mr. and Mrs. Wright and to witness Mr. Wright and the apprentice architects at work.

Before leaving to continue our journey, we asked Mr. Wright if he would someday design a house for us. His answer was yes.

During the following three years, Mr. Wright came frequently to New York City to lecture and to exhibit his work. We entertained him in our one-room apartment at Columbia and expanded our ideas of an ideal house. In Fieldston, on the Horace Mann School campus owned by Columbia University, we found an attractive piece of property. After we persuaded seven young colleagues at Columbia to join us, we presented a proposition to the trustees of the university to lease us four acres. We wrote Mr. Wright a cautious letter describing the possibilities.

After a year the trustees notified us, however, that the university was developing other plans for the property. This was a disappointing setback, but we continued to collect material on houses and furniture and drew conventional floor plans *ad infinitum*. At that time we were intrigued by the work of Le Corbusier, whose style was novel. We were looking for something "modern."

We longed almost subconsciously to return to our western beginnings. (In New York, *western* defined any territory west of the Hudson River.) Early in the 1930s Paul was invited to teach in the summer session of Washington State University at Pullman. This was a big venture. We drove —a seemingly endless trip, but one filled with new experiences. After a rewarding summer we drove south to look at Stanford University, of which we had heard conflicting reports. We found it a paradise in contrast to New York City.

University work at Columbia and the prospect of our first child pushed building plans into the background. Four years and three children later, Paul was invited to spend the summer as visiting professor at Stanford. Jean joined him at the end of the summer session, met the faculty, and got a real feeling for the institution. We did not suspect that this was a probationary episode. However, early in 1935 Paul was invited to join the Stanford faculty. We were overjoyed. We made two phone calls: one to Stanford accepting the appointment, and one to Mr. Wright asking him to think about a house for us in California. Somewhere along the line interest in Bauhaus and Le Corbusier had faded.

In June of 1935 we left New York for Stanford, our ears ringing with the dire predictions of our Columbia colleagues: we were destroying ourselves professionally, recklessly abandoning the East with its great cultural advantages for the frontier West.

We stopped en route at Taliesin and spent three exhilarating days with the Wrights. While Mrs. Wright and the apprentice architects took charge of our three babies, we talked house with Mr. Wright. Together we evolved a set of requirements:

Land on the brow of a hill, with view and drainage, large enough for gardening, playing, and privacy;

A house nestling into the contours of the hill;

A house enclosing enough space for a variety of human activities without crowding three young children and the parents;

A house warm and dry in inclement weather, but thrown open to the breezes of terrace and garden when desired;

Walls of glass so that we could always be visually conscious of sunrise or sunset, the fog banks rolling over the hills, or trees and grass in the fields;

A house so equipped that electricity, natural gas, and labor-saving devices would do the drudgery, leaving time and strength for the more creative aspects of life. We wished to be free of tending the furnace, regulating room temperatures, washing dishes, carrying out garbage;

Furnishings that carried out the simple, unified pattern of the house as a whole; little decoration as such; only the honest use of materials;

A house accommodating art objects that had special meaning for us and reminded us of great events, great people, or great experiences;

A house sheltering indoors up to thirty guests at dinner parties; up to one hundred guests for musical evenings, receptions, cocktails, or teas; overnight guests or relatives; seminar groups of students or colleagues;

A house with terraces and gardens that would accommodate up to two hundred guests for informal functions, sunning or relaxing in sunshine or shade, and children's activities, such as rollerskating, games, dancing;

A house that could be remodeled easily as changing family composition and function required.

We arrived in Palo Alto in the middle of June and settled into a rented house. We fell in love all over again with the lovely village with its five thousand souls and the rolling hills of the Stanford campus.

CHAPTER TWO

Planning Our House—1935/1936

I N late 1935 Mr. Wright began to design our house; in a matter of weeks a perspective sketch arrived. With eagerness and anxiety we unrolled the drawing; we found a rendition of a magnificent two-story house! No accompanying explanation! What to do? Jean was recovering from a fall down a flight of stairs, and Paul was adamant: only a one-story house would do.

Nothing in our archives throws light on why Mr. Wright sent us a drawing of a two-story house. He had not yet seen Stanford nor had we sent him any suggestions on site or design. Possibly this sketch was meant to show us another example of his work. We realized that in some matters the clients' preferences take precedence, so we returned the sketch. We hoped Mr. Wright would understand. He did.

We had been pressing the university unsuccessfully for a decision on possible building sites. A letter of January 29, 1936, explained our site problem to Mr. Wright:

. . . the administration is trying to decide whether . . . to tap . . . the . . . water . . . in the Sierra Mountains or to develop another lake here. . . . If the former, . . . new development will be on one side of the campus; if the latter . . . it will be on the opposite side. . . . I am told that within the next two weeks or a month the water source will be settled, and then we will be able to select our lot.

. . . In case you are in the West and we are able to make a definite decision on the location of our building plot, would it be possible for you to come to Stanford to talk more specifically with us concerning plans and to look over the property? We would like very much to start building next fall.

I have hopes that arrangements can be made for you to give . . . at least one lecture here on the Stanford campus.

On February 11, Mr. Wright answered:

I am glad to hear you are still stalking your lot. We are now at Chandler at the Hacienda and would like to see Leland Stanford. If you would like to come here also we would be glad to show you some houses we are doing and our desert.

In March we could wire Mr. Wright:

INVITE YOU AND YOUR FAMILY TO SPEND WEEKEND MARCH 13 WITH US IN PALO ALTO. READY TO DISCUSS PLANS. WIRE COLLECT.

The Wrights had to suggest a later date, and we wired an invitation to them for the last week of the month. Mr. and Mrs. Wright and daughter, Iovanna, were our guests in our rented home. Mr. and Mrs. Wright were able to observe our children as they played with Iovanna; to note our habits of housekeeping, family cooperation, recreation; and to learn about our research, writing, and teaching. Moreover, we showed Mr. Wright three possible building sites.* Although we all preferred the same alternative, the university authorities declared that no buildings would ever be permitted on those open hills!

As a consequence, Mr. Wright would tentatively design a house for the flat lot, but plans could be modified if we later persuaded Stanford to open the preferred hillside area. At the end of March Mrs. Wright wrote us from Scottsdale:

. . . I am sorry I had to feel ill while visiting you at your home. Thank you so much for your kindness to me and your hospitality. I am well again, and we are starting for home tomorrow or day after. We are coming back in December, since we bought lots of desert and the mountains about 17 miles from here! We will see you, and I will assure you of much pleasanter visit the next time we are together. Best wishes.

After the Wrights' visit a new set of floor plans arrived. Another shock! The designs appeared to be exercises in geometric patterning. During the March visit at Palo Alto, Mr. Wright talked about his hexagonal concept, but our memories do not retrieve any details of these discussions. We recall that we were fascinated at the time but not prepared to comprehend the complex and unconventional geometric grid. Mr. Wright's accompanying letter urged us to study the plans carefully and in depth:

April 2, 1936

The sketches, rather completely worked out, left for Palo Alto today.

I imagine they will be something of a shock, but perhaps not. They will probably explain themselves, but I should mention that the laboratory kitchen is sunlit from above as are the bathrooms and entry toilet.

The [exterior] accordion walls are shown partly moveable but all could be moveable. There is so much glass surface that the tracery of wood crossing the glass makes only a delicate screen wall—leaving tremendous visibility.

* A flat lot beyond Lagunita Court; a sloping lot on the west side of Foothill Boulevard; and a beautiful sloping lot later to be our site on Coronado Street. (Coronado Street was renamed Frenchman's Road several years later.)

I hope the unusual shape of the rooms won't disturb you because in reality they would be more quiet than rectangular ones and you would scarcely be aware of any irregularity.

The furniture works into the scheme naturally enough.

You have contrasting low and high ceilings in every room.

While the plan is spacious and spreads itself, it is not unduly extravagant, I think.

There is a small cellar for heater and storage under the kitchen, entry, and study connecting with the chimney and an outside stairway. The plumbing is well blocked together.

There is no back door—only a bypass for convenience. The "back door" has gone with the "upstairs."

You will see, I think, a very direct pattern for simple living in the dining and working arrangement as related to living room and play space and terraces and garden. There is only a screen for the garage. And the garage floor and fore-court are colored gravel to be raked occasionally.

The house itself is built upon prepared ground—precast hexagonal-unit tiles laid down on concrete and the house erected on the intersection lines.

The outside walls are only 2¾ inches thick of redwood insulated with aluminum foil. The walls inside, just the same, and the ceiling all wood, also worked out on unit lines. Such walls would not burn and the house would be comparatively vermin proof. No termites could work.

I hope you will both like it as much as I do when you become familiar with its somewhat unusual proportions.

It is so much more practical—I believe—than the conventional house that you will find little comparison.

You will see in the plans the *thought* that is *architecture* modern or old.

On April 7 we replied:

Saturday afternoon we received your letter indicating that the house plans had been sent. Naturally we spent a miserable [weekend] trying to wait patiently for them to arrive. They arrived this morning. . . . Our first reactions are most favorable.

As we study the plans in detail, we see certain points at which we wish to make suggestions for slight modifications or changes. We hope to spend a good deal of time this week thinking about these plans.

One of the features with which we are not satisfied is the sleeping arrangements for the children. We are of the opinion that as they grow older each will want his own separate room. That is a problem, however, that we think could easily be taken care of in the general plan. There are a few other minor features which occur to us at the moment, but I will reserve all of these suggestions until I see you in Spring Green.

Paul spent two days at Taliesin with Mr. Wright and the apprentices examining plans on the drawing boards and commenting on them. Many questions had naturally occurred to us because of the unorthodox hexagonal grid and because we had never translated blueprints into reality. Not until the arrival of *General Instructions to Builder* much later, on December 2, could we understand how the geometry of the grid would control many construction phases.

On May 13, Mr. Wright's secretary, Eugene Masselink, advised us:

Here is the floor plan of your house and also your notes with notations by Mr. Wright. We are sorry that they were so long in getting to you but the delay was caused by so much, too much, work in getting settled down to work after the exciting return trip from Arizona.

In late May, we had not received word from the university on a site. On June 5, we wrote Mr. Wright:

As you know, we have been working for . . . months to get a decision from the administrative offices of Stanford as to which lot would be assigned to us for building. Assurance has been held out that our desires for building site could be filled and yet no decision has been made. . . . We have worked long and joyfully over your plans only to find that we must postpone the final stages.

We will communicate with you the moment we are given a lot. Plans will have to be modified then in terms of the new site and detailed plans drawn. In the meantime we will continue to gather our best thoughts concerning the detailed modification of the present tentative sketches.

Meanwhile we encouraged our dean, Grayson Kefauver, to build next to us. The two men planned an attack, to gain the desired lots. One week, Kefauver would call upon President Ray Lyman Wilbur while Paul would approach Comptroller Almon Roth, each presenting a rationale for building on our cherished sites. The following week Paul would present a few additional points to President Wilbur and Kefauver would speak to Comptroller Roth. After several such sessions, President Wilbur said to Paul, "We would save considerable staff time if we allowed you and Kefauver to build on your desired sites." Paul's answer was an emphatic, "Yes, sir!" Whereupon Wilbur picked up the phone, called Roth, and said, "I recommend we allow Kefauver and Hanna to have the lots on the east side of Coronado Street."

Finally, on July 1, we were able to wire Mr. Wright:

TODAY, UNIVERSITY ALLOTTED US WONDERFUL SOUTHERN EXPOSURE HILLTOP SITE. TOPOGRAPHICAL PLOT PLAN READY NEXT WEEK. HOPE WE CAN GET INITIAL SKETCHES PLUS DETAILED PLANS PLUS MODEL COMPLETED SO WE CAN BEGIN BUILDING THIS FALL. ADDITIONAL CHECK ENROUTE.

Looking west from center of site, 1936

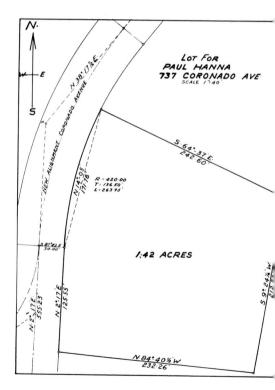

We continued to bombard Mr. Wright with requests for changes, and we seem to have expected immediate action! Today we can see that we pressured our architect unmercifully. Furthermore, we had no legally prepared contract with Mr. Wright. The only document we have is this statement written in pencil by Mr. Wright:

MEMO OF AGREEMENT

It is hereby agreed that Paul Hanna retains the services of Frank Lloyd Wright as architect in the erection, furnishing + planting of a dwelling at Stanford University, California, on a plot of ground to be decided upon for the purpose. The terms of employment are as follows—

For preliminary sketches payable when accepted or rejected by Mr. Hanna, 3% of proposed cost of dwelling.

For plans and specifications, payable when plans are ready, 5% of price of estimates.

For superintendence arranged to mutual satisfaction of parties hereto— 2% of projected cost payable when building is [completed].

Total fee to be adjusted at completion of building.

This document was not dated or signed, yet the trust of all concerned assured that the planning and construction could proceed.

The financial reality of such an unorthodox structure became apparent with the receipt of Mr. Wright's first bill on May 31, 1936:

I am always sorry to bring up the doleful subject of money—but. . . .
By the rules you now owe your architect the preliminary fee of 3½ per-

cent of—we'll say $18,000—$630 to be exact.

If you can manage to send it soon you will know what it is going to do here because we are in the midst of trying to make things grow up!

I hope you are all well and prospects brightening for our mutual enterprise.

We had stated in the beginning that the house cost would have to be limited to $15,000, and we naively thought this would include the architect's fees. Now we discovered that the estimated cost would be $18,000 plus the 10 percent architect's fee of $1,800. We were uneasy over a projected cost of almost 33 percent more than we had budgeted. On June 14, we wrote to Mr. Wright, enclosing a check and questioning the cost and the percentage due. Mr. Wright's response was dated June 17:

I appreciate your dilemma. Everything gets down to a money matter so quickly.

Can we avoid it?

I am sorry, but you are wrong about the preliminary fee. I took pains to elucidate in Palo Alto: I am in this situation in that respect—$\frac{3}{5}$ of my work and all other work is done when I make $\frac{1}{4}$ inch scale plans for one of my houses. You have seen them and know. They are by no means the "preliminary sketch" of the average architect. His preliminary fee doesn't fit our case to such an extent that we have planned to switch the two first fees as they now stand. That is to say, five percent for design as we have to present it, if we present it our way. And I know that is the only way we can adequately present it. Three percent for plans and two percent for superintendence. Also, our total fee has grown too small. My son's fee is fifteen percent. His father still works for ten percent, because that was his fee twenty years ago.

Now this division doesn't represent the relative importance of the various steps, but the amount of our effort and cost concerned in each.

Superintendence is, of course, vitally important, and a member of the Fellowship would be with you on the job as long as you wanted him, on the terms that one is on now in Pittsburgh with Kaufmann, one in Marquette with Mrs. Roberts, and one soon in South Dakota with Bob Lusk. That is to say, as clerk of the works—owner keeping him and paying twenty-five dollars per week to the Fellowship. My personal attendance is yours whenever needed—traveling expenses only added to fee.

I thought you might be your own clerk of the works after we got you started, but the sum involved is small anyway. You might prefer the continuous clerk of the works.

About the preliminary fee you must have misunderstood me, or I misunderstood myself. But don't you worry over that "division." It will come out right in the end anyway.

As for some shift in the lot affecting the plans: I can't see that it can (unless you change the region), that it would be a matter of no more than the grade line on the drawings—which means no other change at all in the plans.

If the sum due, as presented to you, inconveniences you at the moment, take your time and send it in to "the works" at Taliesin when you can.

We are busy and pushing on. I got tossed [off] the road grader making our new road to Hillside. Wrenched neck and leg—couple of ribs knocked in—damn'd painful as I sit here writing, but worse when I try to lie down.

My best to Jean and the babies. If she doesn't want to try my [bedroom] experiment with them, we will fix them up as she wants them at the start. But it would be just as easy (and as cheap) to do it later on a larger scale.

We are all disappointed that you aren't "at it" this fall! Personally, I love that house. A young architect from Edinborough put it before everything else when he assisted us a short time ago.

The amount of the fee had been discussed several times. Mr. Wright had forgotten he had previously set 3 percent as the initial payment. We were grateful that he was charging us only 10 percent; some architects were charging as high as 15 percent.

We were aware that Mr. Wright was doing far more detailed designing on our house than customary, because this was said to be the first residence ever to be built wholly on the 120-degree angle. Without precedent, many construction problems had to be thought out afresh. Because of the much greater effort and time consumed on our work, Mr. Wright could properly have asked us for a 15-percent fee.

We had stressed with Mr. Wright that our idiosyncrasies should be reflected in our home, and we were frank with him in rejecting some aspects of the general plan. For instance, Mr. Wright wanted a single bedroom to serve all three children, with screens between the beds, but his recollection of our youngsters as quiet little angels was not typical of them.

We took a firm stand in a letter of June 21, 1936:

. . . we believe that each family has to work out its own salvation . . . or else go to pieces. For us, the simplest way to achieve . . . harmony as a family is to hold fast to the . . . principle that each individual must have his right to complete privacy. Father has his sanctum, Mother can shut herself up in her bedroom, and each child, from earliest infancy, must have a room where he can be by himself completely, for at least a wee small part of the day. Our whole philosophy of living revolves about the idea of respect for the privacy of other members of our small society. We don't feel that we can nurture that in a situation which sets the stage ideally for one child to waken the others in the morning by rattling a screen, peering around it, or even calling back and forth. This is a bit garbled but perhaps you get the idea. Anyway, we are sure you will get the idea that we are firmly set against any arrangement but that of three separate sleeping rooms for the children.

Eventually we developed a plan to provide a separate bedroom for each

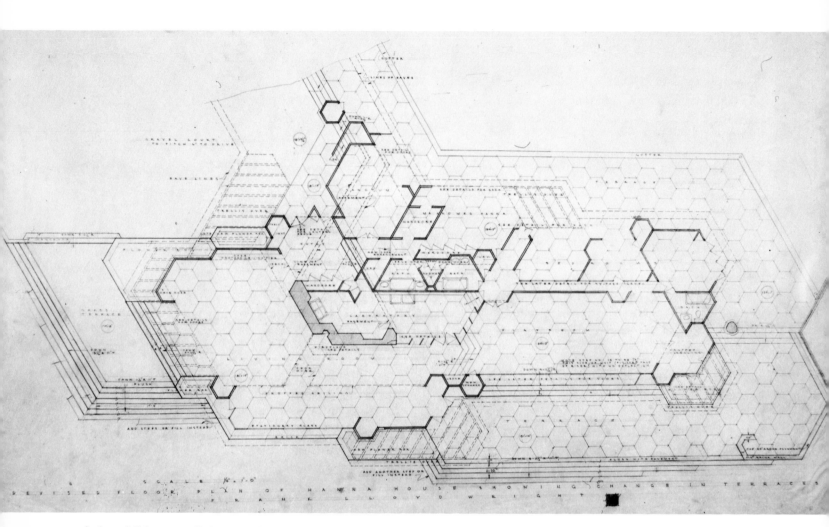

of the children until later, when they would leave us and establish their own homes. Then we would remove nonbearing interior walls between their rooms, creating fewer but much larger spaces for ourselves.

We also asked for a better solution to the dining table, one less disruptive of the living room. But that was not all; we again presented our thoughts to Mr. Wright on July 1:

Inasmuch as the garden watering system for Stanford is polluted, we believe that we ought to have an outside drinking faucet for domestic water.

Where would you suggest telephones? We would like one in the master bedroom and probably the other in the kitchen at the work table. This should be sufficient, we believe.

We would like to have your ideas on a lighting system for the driveway, carport, and grounds.

Original plan, 1936. Bedrooms and steps were changed later. Carport is not shown.

. . . A prospective client is coming to see our house plans this afternoon. Whenever we find a Wright enthusiast—people are by and large too chained to tradition to appreciate your work—we simply let loose and talk freely and joyously of the work you do. If and when our friends sell their home in Fresno, we have an idea they would like to build a small home to retire in. We shall show them the pictures of the Willeys' home.

How we wish you weren't so far away. There are so many things we would like to talk over with you. It would be so nice to be able to bubble over to you when our enthusiasm becomes so great that we almost burst with excitement. We feel repressed because we know we may bore our friends with our enthusiasm.

Expect it won't be long until you will be wending your way westward. In the meantime we hope we will have started our project.

More plans arrived on July 20. We studied them closely. We made copious notes, many of them on the blueprints, spelling out our positive reactions and our doubts or disagreements. When we returned blueprints with comments, we accompanied them with letters. Although each communication to Mr. Wright went forth with trepidation, not knowing what he would say, we continued to pressure him by letter and telegram. On August 1 we wrote:

We find ourselves growing with the house; it's the kind of house that continually challenges one's interest. . . .

We are quite torn in our desires concerning the guest house. Although we feel that it adds materially to the concept as a whole, still we are reconciled to giving it up at least for the present if the total cost is going to be prohibitive. Therefore we are rather positive in our desire to have the daughter's bedroom with private bath as indicated, in order that we may use it as a guest room. . . .

We know that you would be delighted if you could see our hilltop which we worked so hard to get. It really is a gorgeous spot and in ever so many ways is more suitable than the [other] sites that we showed you in the spring.

Mr. Wright answered on August 28:

My dear Jean—Paul (Richt, but not Richter):
The revised plans are with you by now and you have had time to realize "what a virtuoso" your architect had to be to arrange all so completely on a fast slope when it was originally intended for a very slow one. Not easy—but I like the lot, however, and I like the house as well now as before, or better, with the changes in level. The exterior has gained. But the slope has inevitably increased our initial outlay for digging and filling and terraces—about $1,000. No matter what house we built this would be true of a sloping lot.

We lose the old tree that is about lost anyway but the others come in so well that it looks as though we built them with the house.

I think the children well off—better than you had them—and the gallery from kitchen to garden no less than inspiration.

I put in the study fireplace as, if we are going the whole hog, we might as well pay the postage? I hope there will be no further changes now. The thing seems about perfect. When do we "get away and begin?"

Our wire to Mr. Wright of August 31 expressed appreciation for the revised plans, but again asked for "more."

RUSH MODEL BEFORE PROCEEDING WITH WORKING PLANS. . . . DISCOVERED MAN WE BELIEVE TO BE RIGHT SUPERVISING BUILDER. WIRE COLLECT YOUR ESTIMATE OF TIME TO MAKE MODEL ALSO TO COMPLETE DETAILED WORKING PLANS.

Mr. Wright replied on September 2:

CANNOT MAKE MODEL NOW BUT MAY DO SO NEXT WINTER. SKEPTICAL OF ANY CONTRACTOR. BUT IF YOU WANT US TO GO AHEAD WITH PLANS HE CAN GIVE US AN ESTIMATE. NEED THREE WEEKS TO COMPLETE PLANS.

Our answer on September 3 was:

PROCEED WITH WORKING PLANS. UNIVERSITY INSTALLING UTILITIES NOW. DELIGHTED THAT COMPLETE PLANS WILL BE READY IN THREE WEEKS. THRILLED AT THE HOME YOU HAVE CREATED. TIME WILL PASS TOO SLOWLY UNTIL WE CAN MOVE IN.

There seemed no immediate prospect of Taliesin providing us with a three-dimensional model of our projected house, so we built a very crude one using thin wooden berry boxes, Scotch tape, cellophane, and Paul's boyhood erector set. We "walked" through our model and were surprised to discover the mobility the 120-degree angle gave us. We also learned that strange can be beautiful.

As we reread the correspondence exchanged over forty years ago, we wonder how Mr. Wright and the apprentices ever completed the drawings; we were never finished with questions and requests for changes. If we had been planning an orthodox right-angle house, both the clients and the architect would have faced a much simpler set of problems. The following correspondence illustrates the complexities of pioneering.

September 12, 1936

We are hastily dashing off this note in the hope that it will arrive in time for you to consider a few minor suggestions. As we indicated in the telegram, we are thrilled by the house you have created for us. No doubt you have already taken care of many of our suggestions. We send them along now merely to indicate the direction in which our minds are working. . . .

Would it be possible or advisable to have the following doors slide into the wall in order to save space and also to minimize the effect of so many doors? We dislike doors. And yet they are necessary to cut out sight and sound at certain periods of the day. When the door is not needed and can be slipped back into the wall, we think it adds to the illusion of free space.

—Door from master bedroom to gallery

—Door from hallway to daughter's bedroom

—The doors into the lavatories for master and boys' bedrooms

Is the stairway to the basement sufficiently wide? You know our fear of dark narrow stairways and hallways. How will the fireplace chimney in the sanctum alter this basement stairway in the event that we . . . build the fireplace?

Could there not be a small doorway leading directly from terrace walk into garage with a few steps leading down?

We notice the very narrow hallway between the playroom and the children's bedrooms. How can this be widened to a minimum of 32 inches without altering the plans? . . .

We offer this suggestion in reference to the arrangement of the beds in the guest [and maid rooms]: We feel that a bed built with its long axis against the wall gives more of the appearance of a studio couch in the living room. The maid, in particular, will have to use her room as both sleeping and living room. . . . As such it ought to be furnished as a living room rather than a bedroom. The same reasoning might apply to the guest room.

As we understand it, specifications will include every jot and tittle that goes into this structure.

On the basis of these [details], contractors can tell us approximately how much this building will cost. In your telegram you indicated that the working plans may be ready in three weeks. . . .

Do you [not] think it highly desirable for you to be here for a week at the time the contracts are let, or, in the event that we do not use a contractor, then be here to start this project? In case you think it advisable to be here, what week would you propose to spend with us? We need to know this as soon as possible so that we can keep our calendar clear for that time. . . .

On October 15, we wrote Mr. Wright:

Children never had as difficult a time waiting for Santa Claus as we are having waiting for plans. We spend most of our waking moments and a good share of our sleeping time anticipating their arrival. . . .

What are your reactions to our suggestion . . . that you be here to assist in making the contracts and settling a number of last minute details? Unfortunately, Paul will be away from the 17th of October until November 1. After that there are only two months left in this quarter, which Paul took off to build our house. We do hope that we can make a major start on the house before Paul has to go back to the classroom at Stanford.

On October 20, Eugene Masselink wrote us:

The boys have been busy at work to complete your plans as Mr. Wright has finally drawn them. They will be sent to you in ten days immediately upon Mr. Wright's return from the East where he is on a short lecture tour.

November 13 arrived and still no plans. We did not realize that Mr. Wright's accident with a tractor in June had been so severe that he was unable to work much of the time. The letter to Mr. Wright that follows was sharp in tone:

. . . we are at a loss to know why you have not written us giving the reasons for the delay. Surely the few suggestions, all of a minor character, which we made could hardly account for a delay of nearly two months over the estimated time. An encouraging word from you from time to time would have saved us from feeling that our plans have somehow fallen by the wayside.

We wrote you on three different occasions asking specific questions, the answers to some of which are necessary in formulating my own calendar for the autumn. The only answer from Taliesin has been a brief note from your secretary dated October 20, indicating that you were away on a lecture tour and stating that the plans would be sent to us within ten days—that is, November first.

No, we haven't lost faith in our architect, but it is increasingly difficult for us to reconcile ourselves to both the silence and the delay. We appreciate the magnitude of the task involved in creating an experimental house as unique as is ours, but we would like to have the satisfaction of knowing that everything possible is being done to expedite the completion of these plans and to feel that our questions, however trivial, will be answered.

You may recall that we set April 1, 1937, as the completion date for this house. During the past two weeks we have asked our landlord for an extension of our present lease to June 1, 1937. A further extension will not be granted due to the plans which the landlord has made for the disposal of this property we are now renting.

When do you anticipate our receiving the complete working plans which include all details and specifications necessary for bids and beginning of actual construction?

In what manner and when do you intend that we indicate choice of bath fixtures and hardware?

What are your plans for personal supervision of bids, contracts, and soil-turning ceremonies?

We must know at once approximately when you are to be here so that we can set our own calendar to avoid any possible conflicts.

Perhaps at this point in our letter you may gather that the Hannas are slightly peeved at their architect. Well, we might be were it not for the suspicion lurking in our minds that you may have been sitting up nights working out a thousand and one ingenious and lovely innovations which will completely overwhelm us with joy when we finally receive the plans. Maybe, even, you have torn up several sets of plans as you have been inspired to create a more perfect conception.

And so we await word from you. We feel the same eagerness for the arrival of the plans and [for] the day when we begin operations on our hillside.

Again, on November 27, we wired Mr. Wright:

PLEASE MAKE SPECIFICATIONS VERY COMPLETE FOR ALL TYPES MATERIALS AND CONSTRUCTION DETAILS INCLUDING MASONRY, CONCRETE, WOOD, GLASS, METAL, HEATING, PLUMBING, AND LIGHTING. MUST HAVE THESE TO SATISFY UNIVERSITY REQUIREMENTS AND FOR FIGURING COST OF HOUSE. PLEASE RUSH THESE SO WE CAN GET UNIVERSITY REACTION BEFORE PAUL COMES TALIESIN DECEMBER THIRTEENTH. PLEASE COMMENT BY MAIL ON SUGGESTIONS MADE IN OUR RECENT CORRESPONDENCE MOST OF WHICH YOU HAVE NOT INCLUDED IN PLANS.

Mr. Wright replied on November 28:

OKAY. COMPLYING WITH REQUEST.

How could Mr. Wright respond to our telegrams and letters with so little emotion?

———————————

On a Sunday afternoon we were on our hillside lot with plot plan, floor plan, stakes, string, and measuring tape, busily laying out our house among trees. We were so engrossed in our project that we did not hear approaching footsteps. A voice startled us with, "Young people, what are you doing?" We looked up to see Bailey Willis, world-famous geologist, looking disapprovingly at us and our equipment.

We proudly showed him our plans. His reaction was dismaying. With an impatient wave of his hand he said, "You can't build here; a minor earthquake fault runs right through this hill."

"But Professor Willis," we countered, "the university has granted us this site on this hilltop and our architect is drawing up the working plans."

"In that case," said the professor, "I suggest you inform your architect that there is a branch of the San Andreas fault running through this hill." With that, Professor Willis continued his Sunday walk. Naturally we were distraught, and telegraphed to Mr. Wright. We received this reply:

I BUILT THE IMPERIAL HOTEL.

A letter from Professor Willis on September 7, 1936, helped to reassure us:

In the role of good neighbor I should, I think, inform you regarding certain geologic conditions that you might wish to consider in building on your house site. You may, perhaps, not be aware of them.

The rock which underlies most, and possibly all of your lot is a firm sandstone and an excellent foundation for all conditions. But just west of it is a bed of greasy, gypsiferous clay which becomes very slippery when wet. If any part of your foundation rests upon that clay, it should be set in a deep trench and thoroughly drained.

Furthermore your architect should give special consideration to earthquake resistant construction, since a minor earthquake fault runs through the hill, along the western slope. The fault is not itself an earthquake generator, but it may vigorously transmit a shock from the major fault. Being aware of this condition I would, myself, make my residence as light and rigid as possible, would set it on a continuous concrete foundation, and take special care in building chimneys.

There is no occasion for alarm, but good reason for care in design and construction. If you care to talk the problem over, I shall be glad to do so at your convenience.

We were sure that Mr. Wright had already incorporated the major ideas suggested by Professor Willis, but we were grateful for his helpful concern.

We had shown early plans to several contractors and invited them to bid. They declined. They could not understand the hexagonal-module pattern; there were not enough firm decisions on floor plans, elevations, and materials on which to estimate the costs; and rumors persisted that the clients and their architect were probably "baloney."

As an alternative we were thinking of employing a supervisor with building experience who could aid us to find subcontractors, order materials, boss the crews, and keep the accounts. Mr. Wright thought this plan might work if he found that he could not spare one of his apprentices to come to stay on the job until completed. At this particular time, Mr. Wright was busy with several major construction projects.

While we were searching for help, Professor Daniel Mendelowitz recommended Harold Turner, who had supervised the construction of his very attractive home. We interviewed Turner and liked him. He had been unofficially consulting with us for several weeks (on plans sent to us by Mr. Wright in July) when he sent us the following letter:

I am mailing this note in the hope that it may reach you before your letter is off to Mr. Wright.

I have given the plans another look-over and find four additional places where we may need more information. They are:

—The special insulation of the walls.

—Lifting doors in the garage?

—Interior steps—should they be of concrete to match floor slab, or brick to tie in with brick work in living room and other places.

—Detailed drawing of pool.

I wish to express my appreciation for the honor you do me in consulting me, and sincerely hope that I may be the one selected to proceed with the work, as I feel that it is more than a mere house or shelter. It expresses personality in every detail, and may I call it a possession for your soul as well as for physical well-being.

We then wrote Mr. Wright:

It happens that Mr. Harold Turner, one of the two men we are considering for supervising builder, is going to the Middle West for the Christmas season. I believe it would be very strategic to bring Turner on to Taliesin for a day or two for you to look him over and if he is acceptable, give him the works. Therefore, I am proposing to spend December 18 through 20 with you at Taliesin. Mr. Turner will be there for at least one of these days.

Turner went with Paul to Taliesin and remained for observation and training. Mr. Wright directed Turner to visit several sites where apprentices were supervising construction. Turner spent time in the drafting room, sat in on Mr. Wright's seminars, participated in discussions at meals, and joined in construction work under way at Taliesin. Wright approved Turner as our supervisor, and we employed him to commence work early in January, 1937.

Mr. Wright, the eternal optimist, was forever encouraging us to push on in the face of difficulties. On December 1 he wrote:

Herewith are the specifications. More copies later on.

They have been well boiled down and none the worse for the high concentrate. Everything of importance except furniture and planting is decided by them so far as estimates go. If anything comes up that isn't clear or covered at all, let me know.

I am sorry we were unable to send them earlier but we have been having one devil of a time since cold weather struck us three weeks ago.

I'll be looking forward to seeing you here . . . and hope you will tarry awhile.

Don't get excited. All will come through right side up, the better for deliberation. I hope the University shares our enthusiasm for your house.

Our method of presenting questions and suggestions to Mr. Wright was perhaps unique. We would type out, in sentence form, our ideas. Mr. Wright's secretary, Gene Masselink, would have Mr. Wright initial his one- or two-word replies, and this material would be returned to us. Here is an example of eighteen questions sent to him on December 2 and Mr. Wright's answers in italics:

Special insulation, the walls in the sanctum? *None.*
Interior steps—brick or concrete? *Concrete.*
Detailed drawing of the pool: *Later (no money now).*
Sanctum and living room fireplace design construction. What kind of brick?
See specifications. Section later.
Interior ceiling finish: *Nu-wood, celotex, or other board.*
Details of hall partition between boys' bedrooms and playroom. *Completed.*
Shutters in laboratory looking out to living room and playroom: *Completed.*
Cabinet details: *Completed.*
Furniture details: *Not yet.*
Front glass door details: *Later.* Also other doors: *1⅜ inch plywood slabs.*
Bathroom wainscoting: *None, wood boards.*
Garage doors—Better rolling or lifting? *None.*
Suggestions for floor finishes—interior and terrace. *Wax.*
Suggestions for roof covering: *Copper foil.*
Suggestions for hardware: *Plain black iron, invisible as possible.*
Suggestions for lighting—both direct and indirect. *See plan.*
Suggest retaining wall of concrete rather than brick: *Concrete faced with brick.*
Details of window lighting kitchen and baths. Glass too small in baths now.
Not so small.

On December 2 we received general instructions from Mr. Wright.

GENERAL INSTRUCTIONS TO BUILDER
Stanford University Dwelling for Mr. and Mrs. Paul R. Hanna
Frank Lloyd Wright, Architect

This building is to be erected upon a concrete mat laid out on a hexagonal unit system wherein the unit lines become the joint lines of the concrete and this mat must be completed before the superstructure is commenced. In the preparation of this mat, the accuracy of the unit layout is most important and the joints must be made to extend two-thirds of the way through the thickness of the mat. To prepare for the mat, remove top soil beneath it to one side of the lot for use later in regrading. Make all necessary excavation and do with it whatever filling is required to bring the undergrade to within eight inches of the level of the finished floor. This undergrade should slope slightly to avoid any possibility of moisture accumulating beneath the floors. At this time such drains as are indicated should be laid and such retaining walls as are occasioned by excavation or filling of the ground slopes should be built up to the level of the mat to make whatever finish with the edges of the mat may be shown on the elevations and sections herewith.

A filling of coarse gravel or equivalent should now be spread over the leveled and graded surface of the ground—the gravel to be raised to within 3.5 inches of the finished floor and in this gravel bed should be laid such heating and plumbing pipes as are indicated on the plans or for which instructions will be given at the proper time.

When this preparation for the mat is complete the concrete may be laid down in the usual manner, all surfaces finished flat with no pitch, jointing the whole on the unit lines as ordinary sidewalk work is jointed, edges slightly rounded. One and three-fourths inches pipe sleeves three inches long are to be inserted at the intersections of the joints in all exterior extensions of the floor mat. In this dwelling, however, a layer of precast concrete slabs 2 inches thick, of the hexagonal pattern indicated, may be laid and leveled on to a bed of fresh concrete: the joints laid close and left open. The zinc or copper weather strips, at all partition lines (see detail) are to be laid in as shown at this time. When the concrete mat is completed all the wood partitions inside and outside are to be set upon these strips along the unit lines. Wherever the wood partitions or walls occur they begin on the weather strip of zinc or copper which has been inserted into the joint lines of the mat when the mat is made. The mat thus completed is the basis upon which any or all of the prefabricated walls, partitions and the fenestration itself may be erected.

The walls and partitions of this building, inside and outside alike, also laid out upon a vertical unit system (see elevations) are to be made up of a core of vertical boards on each side. This will be covered with heavy paper coated with aluminum foil. Over this paper-covering the horizontal board and inserted batten system is to be put on each side as indicated. The wall and partition sections may be thus fabricated at the shop or on the concrete mat floor of the building. In either case they are to be set up and locked at the corners as shown. Thus all walls and partitions will be three boards and two layers of paper in thickness—the paper carried over and around all corners outside and inside.

The fenestration or the window sections (also fabricated upon the same unit system as the board walls) may also all be prefabricated at the shop, glass inserted and hardware put on complete before setting up the sections at the building. Where this fenestration is intended to support the roof, temporary props may be used until expedient to set the prefabricated sections.

In the roof and ceiling construction the hexagonal unit system of the floors becomes a diagonal unit system on the same lines. All the framing of the roof (piece sizes as indicated) will be done on these diagonal lines (see plan) so that ceilings of Nu-wood or of other synthetic may be securely fastened to the framework with little or no cutting.

There will be no plastering in the building.

There will be no painting or staining of any kind.

It is therefore important that all joints be clean and workmanship good.

The framing of the roof is to be covered with matched and dressed common sheathing or ship-lap. Where the roofs extend over occupied rooms, insulation board 0.5 inches thick is to be laid over this sheathing, the insulation in turn covered with one layer of aluminum foil-covered paper all carefully wrapped around corners and secured under the facia of the eaves.

All exposed roof surfaces are to be covered with a light soft copper sheet put on with standing seams running in the direction indicated on plans: three seams to each unit of the construction. There are to be no gutters, no downspouts.

Where brick work is shown the construction may be brick throughout the wall or a brick facing may be laid up each side and concrete poured within the shells thus made. The brick courses are laid out on the same vertical unit system as the board walls. Vertical joints are to be kept close, pointed flush with mortar the color of the brick. The horizontal joints are to be 0.625 inches high, raked out 0.75 inches deep. Fireplace bricks to be laid same way and of same brick. Hearth likewise: bricks on edge.

MATERIALS

CONCRETE: Clean coarse sharp sand and gravel and Portland cement for walls and mat base. Mixture 1–4. Mixtures always used fresh and cured after laying under wet mats or covering of sand kept wet.

For pre-cast slabs or finish surfaces: 1–3, otherwise same (no gravel).

BRICK: Red paving or sand mold—approved. Laid in cement mortar 1–3. Vertical joints close and flush. Mortar same color as brick. Horizontal joints 0.625 inches raked 0.75 inches deep.

WOOD: Core of walls and partitions, common sheathing 0.875 inches thick. Boards and battens to be of sound redwood thoroughly air dried and seasoned stock to be selected and approved by architect. Roof framing of No. 1 common piece stock—sheathing of common ship-lap. Sash, doors and cabinets to be of selected redwood.

PAPER: Heavy aluminum coated or foil covered building paper.

GLASS: Drawn plate. Or polished plate. Cull plate may be used instead—all to be set in putty with wood strips to cover.

SHEET METAL: Roofing 8 oz. copper standing seams well flashed to brick work or upper wood work and counterflashed in workmanlike manner. Flower boxes lined 16 inch deep with 12 oz. zinc lining with pipe drains inserted in walls. Pipe connections and seams water tight.

HEATING: Horizontal welded pipe system laid in gravel bed under concrete floor mat and connected to oil burning boiler in the basement. Heater proportioned to carry 1,200 feet of radiation. Oil supply tank to hold ten barrels. Layout of this system will be furnished by the architect. For purposes of estimate: allowance $850.

PLUMBING: Durham one pipe system non-siphonable traps, or according to the ordinances of Palo Alto.

Fixtures: Porcelain enameled iron: As few fittings showing as possible; exposed fittings to be white metal selected by owner or architect. Allowance for fixtures: $280.

Sewers: Vitrified drain tile carefully cemented joints to sewer in street below or temporary concrete septic tank of proper capacity. Piping diagram is to be prepared and submitted to architect with estimate for approval.

ELECTRICAL WIRING: All according to fire underwriter's rules. Outlets are to be where and as indicated on plans. Wiring diagram is to be prepared and submitted to architect with estimate for approval. A price per outlet is to be given in case additional outlets are put in. The service is to be carried to the building by utility company ready to be connected to the cut-out box where located.

HARDWARE: To be carefully set by the builder but to be selected by owner or architect: Black iron. Invisible type. Allowance for purposes of estimate: $220.

Necessary permits are to be taken out in owner's name and paid by the builder. The builder will assume all responsibility for any violations of city ordinances in the course of the construction of this building including all necessary employees liability insurance.

The builder shall keep the work adequately insured and facilitate inspection by the architect or owner at all times. Such additional information or drawings as may be required by the builder will be furnished promptly by the architect, when requested, as work proceeds.

Good workmanship throughout the structure will be insisted upon. The architect's opinion on this point to be final and binding upon the builder. All instructions to the builder concerning construction or changes in plans or details must have the sanction or authority of the architect before being executed by the builder. And all payments to the builder shall issue upon architect's certificate— 85 percent of the estimated value of work and material in place from time to time as work proceeds or when in the judgment of the architect such payments are proper.

All of the plans, specifications, and details concerning all of this work are the property of the architect and are to be returned to him upon completion of the building or upon his request at any time.

FRANK LLOYD WRIGHT, ARCHITECT
Taliesin Spring Green: Wisconsin: November 30, 1936

An early preliminary drawing

This document proved invaluable to us when we started construction in January. Some instructions were modified during construction by general agreement among architect, clients, and supervisor.

––––––––––––––––––––

Finally, late in December, 1936, we felt we had sufficient blueprints and specifications to justify presenting them to the university comptroller for his inspection and approval. We asked Mr. Wright to come to Stanford to make the presentation.

We had told Mr. Wright that Almon Roth, the university comptroller, had been in charge of all physical facilities for Stanford for a number of years. All changes of existing campus structures and any blueprints for new construction had to be approved personally by Mr. Roth. We were aware that Mr. Roth feared that any Wright building would conflict with his strongly preferred style (Spanish ranch with red tile roofs) and probably would lower property values for existing residences on campus. But Mr. Wright assured us that we need not worry. He was confident that he and Mr. Roth could come to a satisfactory agreement; so a day was fixed for Mr. Wright to come to Stanford.

He arrived the evening before the scheduled appointment. At breakfast the next morning, he suggested that we walk through the inner and outer quads before the ten o'clock appointment. Paul carried a large roll of blueprints and walked a step behind as Mr. Wright strolled meditatively through the quadrangles.

It was clear that he was in a thoughtful mood. He would murmur, "Magnificent. The hand of that master, Richardson. Nothing matches this architecture in quality on any campus that I know." Paul was delighted.

At ten o'clock they walked into Mr. Roth's office, and introductions followed. Mr. Wright, in his most charming manner, said, "Mr. Roth, I cannot tell you what an inspiration it is to stroll through the beautiful inner and outer quads of this campus. No university architecture can compare with what Richardson's associates gave you. It is truly a magnificent architecture." He paused, then continued, "But, Mr. Roth, I would like to take the person who has been responsible in the last decades for destroying the basic plans for the expansion of this campus and hang him from your tallest tree."

Paul watched in horror as Mr. Roth changed his expression from pleasure to anger. Paul, as shocked as Mr. Roth, decided that approval of the plans had suddenly died.

But Paul glanced at Mr. Wright and was confused to note that his eyes were sparkling with humor. Then Mr. Wright said, "Mr. Roth, I will tell you what to do. You give me the commission, and I will restore this campus just as Richardson would have approved."

With this Mr. Wright burst into a joyful laugh. Mr. Roth saw the humor of Mr. Wright's approach and joined in the laughter. He thrust his hand toward Mr. Wright and said, "Mr. Wright, if Hanna wants you to design his house, I will approve your plans without even looking at them."

Thus began a friendship between our architect and Stanford's comptroller, and thus was set in motion our Honeycomb project.

CHAPTER THREE

Building the Hanna House

FINALLY! After five years of dreaming and two years of planning, in the second week of January, 1937, Harold Turner brought his transit to the property and began to stake the boundaries of the house and establish levels for excavation and grading. We made a ceremony of it.

We were building on the brow of a hill that sloped to the west. We needed to excavate many cubic yards of earth to establish floor and terrace levels. Mr. Turner knew a man for the job, and contracted with Mr. Pyle as follows:

The cost of the excavation will be determined by the actual man and machine hours expended on the job.

The laborers will be paid at the prevailing scale, and the machine hours at $2.00 per hour. You are to receive 5 percent of this total for overhead expenditures and insurance.

The sum of $900 is set as the maximum cost to us for a complete job. If any amount is saved, it will be to the benefit of the owner.

As you know, we are ready to commence, and will appreciate having your part of this job underway as soon as possible.

Mr. Pyle operated his small tractor and usually worked alone. The rains interrupted the excavation during January and February for days at a time. Pyle was with us into the spring, and no one could have been more cooperative and patient. After the construction was well along, we again contracted with him to do the finish grading.

A letter from Mr. Wright dated January 2, 1937, brought us startling news. In the beginning we had told Mr. Wright that $15,000 would have to be the spending limit. In December he had raised our sights to $20,000. Now this:

Have seen Turner. Talked with him. Like him and think he may be our man.

But, to avoid later grief I must say that he should not attempt to build our house including furniture and architect's fees for $20,000.

. . . with the [guest] wing [postponed] into the future, and the expensive but perfect adaptation to a hillside instead of a relatively flat site, $3,500 has definitely been added to [the cost].

This can't come down from heaven as things are. Your figures I find of little or no value for this is easily on the basis of such figures not a $35,000 but a $50,000 house.

So I think it only just to say at this juncture that you should brace yourself against a minimum of $23,500 and a maximum of $25,000.

This a promising young man like yourself with a job should not find outside the bounds of reason. But there is always the guest [wing] to come along later if must be. I told Turner I would say these things to you. . . .

And I am sorry the letter was delayed but I was really on my feet only yesterday—New Years—for the first time.

The details are also on the way.

My best to you all in the sunshine. Perhaps I'll manage my way out later.

What were we to do? Abandon the whole project? Ask Mr. Wright drastically to cut the size and quality of the present plans? Ask him to begin anew and keep within the $20,000?

We could accept none of these solutions. By this time the vision of the finished house was established in our minds; no other house seemed possible. Besides, our pride prevented us from acknowledging that we had lacked the wisdom to get realistic estimates of the total costs before asking university approval and hiring Mr. Turner. The fact that no contractor would bid on the house made it difficult for us as laymen to make a realistic cost appraisal. We decided that we would indenture ourselves to the future. We would go ahead and build!

Mr. Wright was not aware of our momentary shock at the $50,000 price tag. Fortunately he was sufficiently recovered from his bout with pneumonia that he could continue with detailed planning.

Though the lot Lease Agreement between Stanford and ourselves had not been completed, we had actually started excavation. In those early days at Stanford, much work was done in a relaxed atmosphere. Once verbal agreements had been made, work was started and the paper work left to later. On January 15, the Lease and Agreement was ready and signed by Comptroller Almon Roth and the Hannas.* The lease was to run for twenty years, renewable at the option of lessee and lessor. The ground rent was set at $100 per year.

It is reproduced on the microfilm.

Our next communication, on January 4, 1937, was from Eugene Masselink:

All of the points you discussed with us during your stay have been taken up by Mr. Wright.

About the heating and lighting ducts: Mr. Wright, as you probably know, favors the hot air system described by you and wants a diagram from the people who will do this work, showing the layout they intend to use.

The mat can be constructed either way the builder wants but the honeycomb pattern must be kept throughout.

Mr. Wright intends to drain the terraces as shown on the plans, into the gravel fill. . . .

The terrace at the end of the living room may be either grass or garden, as you prefer.

The fireplace hearth can be dropped two or more inches below the living room floor level.

As you probably know, Mr. Wright wants to use the hard burned common brick throughout the house.

The driveway need not be more than 14 feet wide.

Expenses prohibit the sanctum fireplace for now.

All of the boards are to be redwood, the battens pine, held in place by screws, and the sash is to be pine.*

All glass throughout must be cull plate: The house would be cheapened in appearance if inferior glass were used anywhere.

Mr. Wright is considering a special inexpensive copper foil for the roofs.

The sanctum walls will be faced with cork.

The bathrooms are light enough and the walls can be enameled if you wish.

Porcelain fixtures are too expensive for the bathrooms and Mr. Wright doesn't think it necessary to conceal the shower pipes and mixer.

Mr. Wright wants to assure Mrs. Hanna that her scheme will be incorporated in the dining table. He wants to use Klearflax rugs in the house. The phones and phone jacks have been accommodated. There will be adequate provision in the kitchen for recipes and accounts.

We have put in three outdoor water outlets (sill-cocks) for hose.

Mr. Wright believes that the ventilation panels in the bedrooms would be an added expense and that regulated catches on the doors would be sufficient.

The lower part of the seats will be hinged, the one in the living room for storing wood. The files and dictaphone will be properly accommodated in the sanctum.

The history of the construction of our house consists of endless discussions resulting in modifications of previous decisions. We believed with Mr. Wright that these modifications were sound, but they were often costly.

---

* Redwood battens and sash were finally specified.

42

Such is the nature of creative enterprise.

The efforts of the architect, clients, and supervisor to translate the new concept of a hexagonal module into feasible, acceptable working drawings for a house contributed to the delays. We cooled our impatience by reminding ourselves that most tasks are usually behind schedule; but in the end the delays are surely justified. A more perfect product will be the result of the delays caused by creative work that goes into the planning.

On January 10, we wrote Mr. Wright a letter urging delivery of more detailed drawings and asking for advice on many questions:

Yes, we are started! We turned the dirt for the first time last Monday in the rain. It has been raining rather steadily for the past three weeks. The heavy machinery will not work in the wet adobe, so there has been no grading done since we officially started the project. We have promise of another rain storm on the way and it now looks as if it would be a week or so before we can get down to work in a big way.

We have made a very good deal with an excavation contractor. He has agreed to do all the cutting and filling on a man-hour cost basis with a top figure of $900. We have several bids on the road surfacing and the finish of the carport and garage floor. The lowest figure is eight cents a square foot or about $500. This means, of course, an absolutely guaranteed A-1 job.

We are having plenty of trouble over the glass. You know the situation caused by the strike in the glass industry. We . . . can get only ten percent off the new plate price for the cull plate. In fact, most of the glass dealers are charging the same for new or cull—80 cents per square foot in the sizes we need. The double strength grade A is 40 cents. We have consulted wreckers as well as dealers. There is not enough cull in any one dealer's possession to fill our job if we should decide to use it. Stocks are very low. Can you pick up cull plate in the east and ship it out? Would broken car lots cost so much for freight that we would save no money? What do you advise? We can't afford the cost of the 80 cents plate, that is clear. Shall we put in plate in the living room and window glass the rest of the house; or might we use plate in the entire front of the house and glass in the entire rear?

We hope that you are able to work out something in the way of an adequate roof covering. The copper prices have gone to over 13 cents per pound in the domestic market. No roof contractor will agree to furnish copper at the present quotation when we get ready to use it. The lowest price we can get is $40 per square. This price is again out of the question for our budget.

What detail is being worked out for the track to carry the moving glass sash?

We must have a total of *seven* sets of plans. You sent us just four. The University requires two sets. We are moving too slowly with subbids unless we have three sets out at a time. This would leave one set for Turner and one for us. In other words—three additional sets of materials previously sent and seven sets of all plans from now on. Could you have the boys take care of this matter?

Approach road started, January 1937

Cutting the floor and terrace levels

Harold Turner, establishing a floor level

43

. . . We are going in to San Francisco tomorrow to select plumbing fixtures and to get two heating layouts.

We wired you several days ago asking for cross sections on the foundation so that we can see just how you plan to have this laid. We need this for immediate work on the retaining walls. We need reinforcing steel instructions. We still wonder whether or not the plan to drain the terrace water directly into the fill is as satisfactory as a slight slope to the edge of the terrace. The vertical drain pipes will be a nuisance: filling up with leaves, obstructing roller skating on terrace, and catching heels of dancing slippers. Draining into the adobe will cause it to swell and probably crack the concrete terrace. Then, too, the difference in cost of the two methods seems to argue definitely in favor of the slope method.

We also wired you for plans showing the framing of the roof. How is the deck trussing to be constructed? How is the joining to be made at the pitch? How is the glass clerestory to be constructed? Trellis? All these details we must have in order to get a close figure on the amount of material needed. The difference between guesses and sound estimates on a number of these items will determine whether we include or exclude such items as the fireplace in the sanctum. . . .

The Nu-wood [for the ceiling] must have additional nailing surface between the rafters. Or do you have some other idea for this? There must be a number of completed drawings which we do not have: cross section of fireplace and chimney; shutters between laboratory, living room, and playroom; lantern and cabinet details.

Turner has a tool house built and the house foundation pegged out. We are waiting for sun and your further details. When do you plan to arrive in Arizona? We are expecting you to come here as soon after your arrival in the West as you can possibly arrange.

We are enclosing a check for seven hundred dollars to apply on account.

On January 11 we sent a telegram:

EXCAVATION STARTED. NECESSARY PLANS MISSING. RUSH SIX SETS. IF SENT, WIRE COLLECT.

Mr. Wright replied:

BLUEPRINTS SENT LAST FRIDAY. BANZAI.

On the same day, Mr. Wright sent this letter:

I am glad you have started, and I believe everything will come out about right. I hope to be along myself later to steer awhile. Meantime, the inevitable: another sum is now due on architect's fee: the sum of $1,000. This will help me to get on my way.

My best to you all. Did you have a "dirt-throwing" ceremony?

Mr. Wright and the draftsmen were busy in Taliesin with those details we needed immediately to proceed with the job. A week later, Eugene Masselink wrote:

The necessary drawing for the foundation and the mat are being sent to you directly from the blueprint company. The framing plan will be sent later.

Time had come to start assembling a construction crew.

Employing carpenters was difficult, but we developed a procedure that finally worked. Paul phoned the union hiring hall each Friday and asked for three or four carpenters to be on the job Monday morning. Construction was slack in 1937, and we were able to get the number of men requested.

On Monday the carpenters appeared, and Turner and we spent time showing them the blueprints and explaining the hexagonal angle. We instructed them to leave their large squares in their tool boxes and handed them 120-degree angle irons that we had fabricated. Skepticism was evident on the faces of most of the new crew members. The blueprints seemed crazy, and who could build without a square-angle iron? The typical carpenter worked cautiously and very slowly on Monday. By the day's end one of the carpenters would quit. By midweek we would suggest to another that his unhappiness with the job justified his finding other work. Turner would pay him off.

By Friday we usually found one or two of the week's crew to be skillful cabinetmakers. We retained them and placed another order for carpenters to show up on Monday following. This process of trial and elimination went on for the first four weeks. Finally we had a crew of seven cabinetmakers who stayed with us for the year. The interest these men took in the construction of a new module building and the skill with which they worked was a joy to behold; they sensed that they were partners in an important architectural innovation.

Our carpenters discovered many ways to translate the blueprints into three dimensions. They constructed a temporary workshop and equipped it with templates and gauges for mass-producing the lumber into boards, battens, and jambs of the proper length.

While waiting for blueprints, and between rains, we continued with site preparation. The plot plan sent in 1936 to Mr. Wright was used by him to locate the buildings in such a way that the white oak trees and the lone cypress on the grounds would not be disturbed. One small oak stood in the center of the living room-to-be, a sickly tree without potential. We decided to remove it. The cypress, a large, bark-beetle-infested tree, stood in the center of the breezeway between the main entrance and the carport. We were concerned about its longevity. The university superintendent of grounds advised us that it would soon die. Not only was the tree infested with beetles, but we would sever its roots when we cut away four vertical feet of earth on three sides to establish levels. However, Mr. Wright drew plans to bring the cypress through the roof of the breezeway and to build a brick wall on the three sides. In 1981, the cypress tree still lives.

The white oaks were badly shaped, roots exposed by burrowing ground squirrels, limbs dying from poor soil and lack of water; some of the larger limbs had rotten heartwood and could easily break in a strong wind.

One of Paul's graduate students, Ronald Linn, had been a tree surgeon with the Davey Tree Company. Ronald agreed to present a plan for treating the oaks; if accepted, he would restore them by cementing the interior of rotten limbs, placing steel cables to strengthen them, and preparing proper drainage basins. Ronald and Paul spent weekends in February and March carrying out these plans. A comparison of photographs taken during the work in 1937 with recent photographs will demonstrate that pruning, cementing, cabling, feeding, and watering over the years made beautiful trees out of the original scrubby specimens.

Upon completion of the tree work, Ron presented a bill for $33.25 for his thirty-five hours of work and travel and expenses.

Mr. Wright early proposed that we heat the house with hot water in copper tubing laid in the concrete mat. This solution for heating a central California house seemed questionable to us. We estimated that the proposed system would take about an hour to heat a room in the morning. When the thermostat registered the proper room temperature and lowered the water heat in the tubes, the heat in the concrete would continue to raise the room temperature for some time. As a result, we thought the room could not be heated quickly enough in the morning and then kept at a comfortable and constant temperature for the daytime. We needed a system to give us quick heat on demand and one that would not overheat after the thermostat recorded the desired temperature.

Mr. Wright also had second thoughts. To that date very few buildings had used this system, and he had incorporated so many innovations in our plans that he questioned the advisability of overdoing the experimental.

The two years we had lived in California had persuaded us that gas-fired hot air was the method we preferred for heating our home. This system required large space for hot and cold air ducts. Paul came up with the idea of constructing a tunnel under the concrete mat, this tunnel to follow the long axis of the house. This would permit connections for riser ducts up through the concrete floor to every room in the house. The underground furnace room would lead into the tunnel.

How large should we build the cross section of the tunnel? We planned to locate all utilities—plumbing, electricity, and heating—in this tunnel. Sewer pipes, cold water pipes, hot water and return hot water pipes, electrical conduits, and the hot air ducts and cold air return ducts had to be accommodated. In addition we would sink our bathtubs in this tunnel; we could make plumbing connections to tubs from within the tunnel. The top of the sunken tubs, being at floor level, would leave more free space in the bathrooms.

We obtained estimates for the cross section of adequate duct size. By placing in the tunnel all utilities and the bathtubs, and allowing crawl space for a person to inspect and repair, we figured we needed a four-by four-foot cross-section tunnel. With Mr. Wright's approval we drew up the detailed plans and dug the trench for the tunnel.

A shipment of a few blueprints arrived the third week of January. But these plans did not give us sufficient guidance to proceed on many jobs. Lacking crucial blueprints and without answers to the numerous questions raised by our letters, we became impatient and even angry. The rains were subsiding, and our crews were not properly busy. We composed a telegram to Mr. Wright that exposed our frustrations, our arrogance, and our shameful lack of compassion for our ailing architect. The text of the wire sent on January 25 was:

MUST HAVE FOUNDATION PLANS IMMEDIATELY. GRADING DONE. WAITING TO POUR CONCRETE RETAINING WALLS. ASSUMED YOU HAD HONORED OUR REPEATED REQUESTS FOR STANDARD BATH FIXTURES, DOORS, HALLWAYS. ON CHECKING LATEST BLUEPRINTS FIND DOORWAY WIDTH 24 INCHES AND LESS, HALLWAYS LESS THAN 20 INCHES, 24 INCH BATHTUBS, 30 INCH BEDS, AND OTHER EQUALLY IMPOSSIBLE LIVING CONDITIONS.

COMPLETE REDRAWING OF BATHROOMS, HALLWAY, AND BEDROOMS MUST BE DONE IMMEDIATELY. WIRE COLLECT WHETHER YOU HAVE TIME TO REDESIGN AT TALIESIN OR WHETHER YOU WILL COME TO ARIZONA WITHIN NEXT TEN DAYS AND IMMEDIATELY THEN TO PALO ALTO.

Would not most recipients of such a demanding telegram have responded by telling us to forget the whole affair? Today, as we read this insulting wire, we are covered with embarrassment. But the wire was sent, and we must confess Mr. Wright would have been fully justified in abandoning his demanding clients.

On January 26 a telegram arrived from Frank Lloyd Wright as follows: SUCH OF YOUR REPEATED REQUESTS AS UNDERSTOOD HONORED BEST OUR MEAGER ABILITY. FOUNDATION PLAN SENT SEVEN DAYS AGO. COMPLETE ROOF FRAMING DIAGRAMS NEARLY READY STOP YES TWENTY FOUR INCHES [BATHTUBS] TWENTY ONE INCHES [HALLWAYS] ARE MY SENSIBLE PRACTICE. DOORS TOTAL LOSS EXCEPT ADEQUATE WAY IN AND OUT. TRY ONE ON SHIP OR PULLMAN SCREENED PASSAGES TWENTY SIX. THE HANNAS LIKE THE WRIGHTS ARE NOT SO BIG STOP BEDS SEE SEARS ROEBUCK TWIN SIZE MODERN THIRTY NINE BY SIXTY SIX PAGE FOUR HUNDRED TWENTY STOP BATHS TWENTY EIGHT INCHES STOCK SEE BATHROOM DETAILS ADAPTING STOCK FIXTURES STOP STOCK AND SHOP PROPORTIONS AWKWARD AND WASTEFUL IN UTILITIES AS AESTHETICS. KINDLY SEND TERMS AGREEMENT WITH BUILDER SO WE MAY PUT IT ON REGULAR CONTRACT BASIS. BEST NOT GET TOO EXCITED LONG WAY TO GO. AM STILL HOUSE BOUND.

Fatherly advice to brattish clients! He tried to reason with us and climaxed his message by urging us to be patient.

But we were not in the mood to be patient or even understanding. We were not protected by a contractor's fixed price. We were paying by the hour regardless of whether any correct work was done. We wanted decisions that would result in action the next morning on the construction site. Within an hour after receiving the above telegram, we sent off the following letter special delivery:

We received your voluminous telegram tonight. Couldn't wait to answer until morning. . . . We were quite prepared to read a telegram which would burn us up. Instead you sweetly turn the other cheek. The only conclusion that we can draw from your telegram is that we must be incredibly stupid in reading your plans. We are perfectly willing to grant that. All we ask is that we be shown wherein and exactly how our measurements of the plans differ from yours.

To proceed directly to the point.

The hallway separating the bedrooms from the playroom is 19.5 inches. The hexagonal block is 45 inches between parallels. One-half of 45 is 22.5 inches. Subtract the 1.5 inches twice for the width of the walls . . . and you have 19.5. Correct? Yes, we may be small people but hardly pygmies. There may be some possibility of turning sideways and sliding through a pullman door, but it is another story when you try to walk sideways for thirty feet. What do you propose? Your telegram speaks of the screened passage being 26 inches. Do you propose to alter the plans 6.5 inches? If so which wall is moved—the bedroom wall or the playroom wall? You see we can't lay the concrete mat until we know *exactly* where the metal strips and the plumbing and electrical outlets come in the fresh concrete.

You speak of tubs for the bath as being 28 inches wide. We have again checked your plan and find them 24 inches wide by 4.5 feet in length. We want the Wrights to spend many happy days with us but we know that they will not stay long if they try to bathe in tubs so short. Further we are ignorant of the fact that you could get tubs in the 24 inch width or the 28 you speak of in your telegram. We will look into this narrow tub tomorrow to see if they can be purchased here. Still the matter stands where it was—we want tubs 30 inches wide and 5.5 feet long. Paul bathed in the washtub in the kitchen too long as a child to get much pleasure out of these smallish fixtures. . . .

Maybe we should get over such traditional notions and learn to live with these procrustean beds, tubs, doorways. But somehow we find it hard to justify 30 inch beds, 19.5 inch hallways, and 24 inch wide bathtubs when we have over an acre of land and a floor space of such spacious size. Couldn't we just cramp the principle an inch or two here and there in so large a field in order to live a little more freely and with more flexibility? We suggest your fight against the stranglehold of tradition and unbending principle, and your insistence that the only true principle flows out of the demands of abundant living, call for relaxing a principle when it is found to be restrictive to life. Are we wrong again?

And so we could go on far into the night. You have created for us a marvelously beautiful home. Of that we are so certain we are willing to stake our all on it. . . . You seem to suggest we are borrowing trouble and that we will find the machine will function smoothly when we finish it. At times our regard for you almost reassures us.

. . . We have sent out the plans for bids on heating and plumbing and will get them back by the last of this week. The electrical plans will be ready in a day or so. We will send you the layout for your checking.

We agreed to pay Harold Turner $300 a month for five months. He agrees to finish the house no matter how long it takes. He gets no more than the $1,500 for his entire services. We keep about $500 cash in his account so that

Wood forms for the construction of the retaining wall, January 1937

Stripping wood forms from retaining walls

The concrete mixer

he can pay for small items as needed. He gives us a statement each week to show the expenditures for that week. We work together on getting the subcontracts but they are written in my name. Turner personally hires and fires the day laborers and the carpenters. So far we have found him to be excellent.

We are much distressed over your condition. What do the doctors say about your trip west? When do you anticipate you will come? Are any of the boys coming to Arizona ahead of you? Would it be wise to have one of them come on for inspection if you can't come yourself soon?

Please take care of yourself. You are more important to us than the house. We know that you will do the wise thing for us. Please rush the remaining plans and answers to our questions.

Faithfully and affectionately,

As we reread this exchange of messages, we are amazed by both the sharp, even abrasive, language of our letters to Mr. Wright and the extraordinary tolerance with which he reacted. This exchange should emend some judgments about the arrogance and intolerance of Mr. Wright. The intolerance and arrogance must in this exchange be assigned to the Hannas.

What was the reaction to our letter of January 26? A reply dated January 27 contained one of the few instances of gentle sarcasm we heard from Mr. Wright:

Following up my telegram: I am afraid the full import of the plans for your domicile hasn't yet penetrated your scholarly brain, and that reality is still to dawn there.

For instance: I tried to impress upon you the fact that stock and shop proportions in planning modern houses were as clumsy and wasteful as they were ugly. Conservation of space based upon the proportions of the human figure has taken place actually so far as I know only in building ships and pullman cars, the Imperial Hotel, and my own houses, although "modern architecture" has done something.

This house of yours is the latest essay in that direction wherein good aesthetics call for adequate but economic treatment of this important matter where living in houses is concerned. The unit we have adopted fixes the minor door openings at 1 foot 10½ inches. See larger scale detail. The door to my own bathroom opens to 1 foot 9 inches. It has not occurred to me that it was narrow. I am sure there are no impossible living conditions anywhere, even in the narrow gallery leading the little girl to her bedroom. That is open above the head—the wall on one side being a mere screen. It is a little discouraging to find you rudely awakened to all this at this time. But architects must learn patience to back up what skill they have, and I can see how this matter of scale didn't get to you.

When I planned the house I expected we would make the beds, having the

Simmons Factory make up the special mattresses at no great cost. The damn beds in stock use are bigger than true comfort demands and make mere stalls out of the sleeping rooms. Only seldom is stock furniture in good human scale. It is my opinion, based upon repeated trials, that springs 32 inches by 66 inches making up into a bed about 34 inches by 72 inches is not too small for comfort. But in order to use the stock 39 inches by 66 inches we simply have to design our bed framing accordingly. This does not change the plan at all.

Now indubitably, when the proportions of doors, furnishings, are measured to the simple requirements of human use, there is greater satisfaction in the freedom to use the whole space. The house seems larger—the rooms seem and are larger while, certainly, physical comfort is no less.

Briefly, this is the thesis. You have heard it from me before. And I am sure when you concentrate on it without too much ring around a rosie and holding of outside hands you will recognize its common sense. Or shall we say science? It is the kind of science that is the true basis for art.

The little girl's corridor is narrow—1 foot 9 inches, and without any re-drawing we can add a few inches if you shy at it.

As they are, the bathrooms are all right for stock fixtures. The tubs should be a type built to the walls and project about 28 inches. The bowls should be ordinary size and free-hung. The seats will be pedestals. And you have plenty of good-looking room.

I have studied this thing all the later half of my architectural life with the idea of the eventual prefabricated house. I *know* what I am talking about. It is no matter of taste but, if it were, good taste is all on the side of more human proportions for articles of human use. Habit is a hard horse to beat, as you know. But you and Jean are yet young, I believe. And the children will grow up with the new sense of things. They will start a little ahead of their parents, therefore, who grew up in the old order and have to turn now and look at it in the face for what it is worth. This is the new reality, Paul. Your house is a factor in it of no mean import if you stand up to it.

Try to get hold of this in the feet and inches of structure as I have.

A bad leg—phlebitis—(pneumonia aftermath) keeps me down, off my left foot. I broke it up in Tokyo while building the Imperial Hotel and it seems a weak place where the strain shows. . . .

Your architect is your protection (which at the moment you do not feel the need, of course). Nevertheless—perhaps for that very reason the agreement should be recorded here in proper terms or we will find eventually neither head nor tail to the effort or be able to locate the middle.

After you have in hand the drawings we have been making to extra illustrate the plans (which will be very soon now) and our builder has digested them, if you feel it necessary, I will send a superintendent to stay with you while you need him. I don't want to promise anything about my own advent. What-ever gods may be take umbrage where there is too much presumption.

I hope this lets in light and restores confidence. If it doesn't why then let those same gods have mercy.

At this end I have investigated the delay in your receiving plans and find the blueprint company at Madison is probably at fault—protestations not withstanding. It may be best to forward originals to you and let you make the prints you need there charging them to us and returning the originals to us promptly.

This January 27 letter is a masterpiece of logic, a declaration that the master knows his art, reassurance that he is our ultimate protector; it contains delightful references to the part that the gods might play in our joint efforts. We were indeed restored in faith.

However, before we had received this letter, we wrote on January 28 as follows:

By now you have doubtless had time to read and digest our letter of January 17. We trust that you will send us a speedy and enlightening answer to the questions and problems raised therein. We must have an immediate answer to the following:

Referring to the problem discussed in the fourth paragraph page two of the January 17 letter—as to prior correspondence and discussion with the boys while at Taliesin: All of us here strongly advise substitution of *slightly sloped terraces* for drainage in place of the 1 inch pipes at intersecting of the blocks. On every count the slope seems superior to the pipes for drainage (for elaboration, see previous correspondence). Please suggest in a pencil sketch the treatment of the edge of the concrete mat including gutters and drain pipe to carry the water run off from the sloping terraces.

We trust that Eugene will have the time within the next few days to send us a written report in considerable detail of your discussion of the problems raised by us in our letters of January 17 and January 28.

We prefer more than a *yes* or *no* answer for "we are from Missouri" and therefore must be shown the reasons for your decisions or preferences as the case may be.

We trust that additional sets of blueprints have been sent us for use in getting subbids on plumbing, heating, and electrical.

The wooden forms for the concrete retaining walls are almost complete. We have rain predicted for the next four days which will hold us up. But we are making progress.

We have a lead on a plate glass source that looks promising.

Two days later we had received the January 27 letter from Mr. Wright. We wired:

NEED IT BE SAID WE HAVE ETERNAL FAITH IN THE MASTER. WE WILL BUILD OUR HOME AS YOU DESIGN IT AND PROUDLY STAND UP TO IT. NOTWITHSTANDING, WE BESEECH YOU TO SATISFY OUR DESIRE FOR UNRESTRICTED MOVEMENT OF HUMAN FIGURES THROUGH DOORS, HALLWAYS, IN BEDS, AND TUBS. WHERE YOU CANNOT DO SO PLEASE APPRISE

US FULLY OF YOUR REASONS. NATURALLY WE EXPECT TO DEFEND 22 INCH DOORS AGAINST LOCAL BUILDING CODES AND INSPECTORS WHEN TIME COMES. PLEASE REVIEW AGAIN OUR SUGGESTIONS, THEN WRITE FINAL INSTRUCTIONS.

Much of our trouble stemmed from the fact that we were slow in comprehending how Mr. Wright created a unit system grid for the floor plan and then made the parts of the building conform to that geometry. Once we grasped his unit approach and no longer thought of doorways and bathtubs in standard shop dimensions, we discovered that his grid did produce space that conformed to the human scale.

Most projects do not run smoothly with a perfect resolution of problems. As we look back on these controversies, we believe the exchanges, painful at the moment, were significant in educating the clients and refining and fine-tuning the plans. The ultimate satisfaction that the clients and the architect foresaw in the finished honeycomb house were powerful enough to take us through these difficult exchanges. One must remember that the clients had been abundantly prepared for difficulties by reading the writings of Frank Lloyd Wright, particularly his autobiography. We believed deeply in Mr. Wright's philosophy from the time we read *Modern Architecture,* his 1930 Princeton lectures. And Mr. Wright was a man of patience who could wait for clients to digest his theory and designs.

Further input from Taliesin helped us see more clearly the beauty of Mr. Wright's honeycomb plan. During the last week in January, a young apprentice who was working on our plans, L. Cornelia Brierly, wrote an article for a Wisconsin newspaper:

At Taliesin a new unit system for designing a house has recently been developed. A unit system is a form of standardization, a regular division . . . of the building space . . . in this case, a hexagon 4 feet 4 inches in diameter. The building is woven on these imaginary lines as a rug is woven on its warp insuring consistent proportion and enabling the builder to take full advantage of repetition. The final application is a spacious honeycomb house designed to suit the needs of the living, growing family of a professor at Stanford University in California. For years Mr. Wright has used unit systems to give order and form to his houses. This system provides for future expansion, holds steady the scale of the building, and is serviceable for mechanized shop fabrication. The unit usually adopted has been a square or rectangle but now comes the hexagon—the practicality of which has been proven by the experience of those master builders, the bees.

53

The sociological structure within the beehive demands a unit adaptable to the tremendous growth and activity that flows on from one generation of bees to another. The bee employs a hexagon as its workable unit. Because of the hexagon's form, its lines follow one upon the other until they become space florescent. And the hexagon's equal angles assure strength and rigidity not only in the single unit but in a collaborative system where every subdivision adds strength to the next—*ad infinitum.*

These properties of the hexagon characterize the glass and wood honeycomb that is the house of Mr. and Mrs. Hanna. Because of maneuverable glass walls the house can be completely opened to the outdoors, letting its living room or playroom or bedrooms or study become a part of the terrace system. In hot sun or bad weather a great expanse of horizontal roof protects this working hive of a lively family. The mother is queen bee of the Hanna Honeycomb and from her kitchen in the center of the hive she can supervise the housework and the activities of her growing young family.

Because the hexagonal unit determines the shape of the concrete mat (the floor of the house) into which the honeycomb's walls are anchored, the addition of future rooms can be natural and easy. Walls of battened redwood boards are lightly constructed and derive their strength not primarily from 1 by 8 inch stud construction, but from the hexagonal conformation of the thin wooden walls with the floor and roof. Yes, the house is completely free from the obstruction of heavy walls, sharp angles, and the usual holes in walls. Under its commodious roofs, interior space is devoted to living.

A clear, inspiring conception relates this California honeycomb house to the climate, the locality, and the human activity of the Hannas.

Although we had heard the same doctrines from Mr. Wright, the reinforcement from this young designer helped us to grow in understanding and appreciation of the honeycomb concept.

On February 2, Mr. Wright wired us as follows:

WISH TO CHANGE LEVELS AND WALLS OF LIVING AND PLAYROOM TERRACES IF NOT TOO FAR ALONG.

On the same day we replied:

NOT TOO LATE TO MAKE THE CHANGES. WOODEN FRAMES FOR RETAINING WALLS JUST COMPLETED. HAULING GRAVEL AND CEMENT TOMORROW. READY TO POUR RETAINING WALL ANYTIME AFTER FRIDAY. PLEASE RUSH NEW INSTRUCTIONS. JOBS MOVING SPLENDIDLY DURING THREE RAINLESS DAYS.

On February 2, we also wrote a letter to Taliesin and enclosed some of the sketches of our proposals for the heating layout. We concluded our letter by pressing for a decision on when Mr. Wright could come to Stanford to help on problems. We were still unaware that he was very seriously ill. His communications to us in the previous days had been interpreted by us as notice that he might come at any time soon:

You will find enclosed two heating layouts: one, blueprinted, submitted by Watrola; the other, a sketch, submitted by Electro-gas.

The Watrola system is forced hot water to three conversion units located in recessed chambers underneath the mat, opening directly into the tunnel. . . . The district engineer of the Watrola company who drew these plans estimates that the finished job will cost approximately $1,600 plus the cost of materials (tile and concrete) and labor to construct the recessed conversion chambers, the tile return duct system, and the risers in the walls.

The sketches submitted by the Electro-gas company are the more usual hot air type and require no comment, except to say that our tunnel would have to be 4 feet by 4 feet cross section to take the number of hot air and cold air ducts. The Electro-gas engineer estimated that this system would cost about $1,500 installed. However, this figure as well as the one indicated above cannot be relied upon.

Will you, after studying these two layouts select one of the following:

Reject both and suggest next steps.

Choose the better and suggest any necessary modifications in layout or specifications.

If you have no preference, suggest any necessary modifications for both proposals, allowing the choice to be determined by the most advantageous bid from heating contractors.

We hope that you will find it possible immediately to airmail these plans back with your specific recommendations so that we may submit plans to several heating contractors for competitive bids.

If you are not coming to Arizona by March 1, would it be possible for you to come from Wisconsin? What are your suggestions?

It seems to me that there are several times when your own presence or the presence of one of the boys may be important:

when pouring the concrete mat and inserting the utilities outlets and metal wall-marking strips;

when we first attempt the construction of a section of wall.

It may be extremely helpful to have you here when we start the roof framing, particularly the section tied into the outside wall of the playroom.

We hope your health is steadily improving.

On February 3, Mr. Wright wired:

SENDING MORE LIBERAL SCHEME SUBSTITUTING CONCRETE STEPS FOR RETAINING WALLS. OTHER DETAILS ABOUT READY TO GO.

Eugene Masselink wrote to us on February 4:

We are sending you drawings *special delivery* in this mail. Notations . . . will answer the questions in your two last letters.

The framing plan will be sent within three or four days.

Kindly send us the original drawing back with one set of blueprints as soon as possible—and send the blueprinting bill to us.

On February 5, Mr. Wright responded to our letter about the heating system:

While I was ill a basement plan went off to you with the basement "in wrong." I hope it is not yet dug because I originally intended to have it at the center of the house next to the chimney to get the full effect of the heater where it would do most good and equalize distribution. But if dug let it go.

The Electro-gas heating system you sent is the better (the other is impossible) but unnecessarily expensive, and we can't put registers above the floor.

Why not try a simple steam blower system with oil burner delivering heated air in ducts to floor outlets—about $800—best?

You don't want the bedrooms above 60 degrees, I hope, and your big fireplace will provide heat as well as aesthetic satisfaction while you burn it in cheerless weather for living room and playroom—so 60 degrees for the whole house so far as heating goes ought to be all right.

These fellows all have terrific factors of safety (ignorance) and crowd in as much as they think the traffic will bear.

Tell the Electro-gas people you have $1,000 to spend and no more. The change in basement location will help some also. The Electro-gas seems a pretty good system but we can't absorb it as they present it. Couldn't they see what they were doing to the house? But why should they care?

We agreed that the "big fireplace will provide heat as well as aesthetic satisfaction" in the living room but could not agree that "60 degrees for the whole house so far as heating goes ought to be all right."

A month later we contracted with Electro-gas Company for a gas-fired, forced-air, three-zone control system, with a capacity to give us 70-degree temperature when we desired it in any part of the house.

On February 10 a letter from Eugene Masselink informed us that special delivery mail would bring us "complete framing details with sections . . . and the complete details for jambs. Details of entry lantern, clerestory windows, and laboratory will follow shortly."

On February 18, we wrote to Mr. Wright:

Your new plan, dropping terrace off playroom and opening living room to play terrace, adding steps to front of house, is beautiful as well as useful. Unfortunately we had the forms built and some concrete poured before the new plans came. Therefore we will cantilever the playroom terrace ½ a hexagon tile out over our present retaining wall. Also we have a very large drop from this terrace edge to natural ground level so we dropped the whole house six inches. From the pictures enclosed you see our "fill" and "steps" problems.

The terrace and grass off the living room is so close to two trees that we can't have steps with fill under if we want to save these two trees. What do you propose?

Rain has held us up the last three weeks—almost continuous rain. As a result we won't be ready to pour the concrete mat before the 10th or 15th of March.

We have postponed signing subcontracts on electric work, plumbing, heating, milling, and brick work until I return to Palo Alto on March 3.

Your sketches have been blueprinted in the engineers' office at Stanford and returned to you. We have sent you one print of every drawing. When I get the bill at the end of the month from the Comptroller's office, I will send it on.

We have purchased the plate glass—the order for which you okayed.

The basement had been dug before your revised plans came. Inasmuch as it is partially in rock and expensive to dig, we have left the basement as dug.

The Electro-gas Company is making a new layout to get within our price limit.

We need more copies of blueprints of certain plates: 3—Revised floor plan—lighting shown (for lighting bid), 4—Revised full-sized details (for milling bids).

Need to see new furniture layout for locating electrical outlets and heating vents.

What decision on the roof covering? Copper went to 14 cents per pound yesterday.

Need details of redwood board and batten wall so we can get a figure from the mill.

Have no document from you as yet of agreement for Turner to sign.

Leaving tonight to be gone two weeks. Jean will handle matters while I am gone.

The *Stanford Daily,* the publication of the Stanford students, carried a story on February 19 that reveals something of the campus interest in the activity on our hill. While minor errors of fact appear, the account does reflect the excitement in the student body.

A dream castle come true is Architect Frank Lloyd Wright's contribution to the Stanford campus and the happiness of the family of Dr. Paul R. Hanna, associate professor of education.

Completed, it will be Stanford's most romantic home situated on Stanford's most romantic spot.

That spot is Pine Hill, undermined by tunnels a half-century old, surrounded by crumbling relics of bridges and dams, and proposed site of the continent's most palacial mansion—dreamed of sixty years ago by M. Paulin Caperon, alias Peter Coutts, better known to Stanfordites simply as "The Frenchman."

Today, plum over the mouth of Coutts' tunnel, foundations rise of what in July will be one of America's most unique homes, planned by perhaps its foremost home architect.

Builder Harold P. Turner claims the house will be 50 years ahead of its time both in design and materials used. Patterned after the honey-comb, it uses a hexagon four feet in diameter as basic unit of design.

Only right angles in the entire building will be where walls and floors meet. Sliding glass door extending across the 117 feet of frontage on Coronada Avenue will enable Hannas virtually to live outdoors, weather permitting.

But most singular of all is the "personality" Mr. Wright has given the construction. Not until he had lived with the Hannas several weeks last spring did he begin the designing.

As a result, every detail in the construction is compatible with the Hannas' likes, philosophies, idiosyncrasies.

"It takes a heap of living in a house to make a home," says Poet Eddie Guest. But when the Hannas move into their new domicile, completely furnished by Wright, it will truly be their home, as like them as themselves!

Around them will be the relics of Frenchman Coutts' story, the unravelling of which has become Dr. Hanna's fascinating hobby. Thirty feet below his basement meanders one of the two old tunnel systems which leads to "Frenchman's Tower" two miles away.

Architect Wright, now recovering from influenza, has been unable to leave his Spring Green, Wisconsin, home to watch building progress. He hopes, however, to visit the Farm for that purpose next month. It will be the third home on the Coast he has designed, the other two being in Pasadena.

Early in March we sent a telegram to Mr. Wright:

PLEASE FURNISH ANSWERS AND DETAILS REQUESTED LETTER OF FEBRUARY 18. WITH NEW HALLWAY WE ASSUME BOYS' BEDROOM FURNITURE ARRANGEMENT IS MODIFIED. MUST HAVE NEW FURNITURE PLAN TO PLACE ELECTRICAL AND HEATING CONNECTIONS THROUGH TUNNEL WALLS AND THROUGH FLOOR MAT. HOW IS YOUR HEALTH? ARE YOU ABLE TO COME WEST?

After some further exchange, Mr. Wright informed us that he, Mrs. Wright, and daughter, Iovanna, would arrive in San Francisco on March 14. We installed them in a friend's house, only one block from our site. Our daughter, Emily-Jean, and Iovanna Wright had high adventure digging for pieces of earthquake-damaged mosaic from the Stanford Chapel, dumped in the old lake bed. Mr. Wright helped answer some difficult questions. Their stay with us was far too short.

On March 20, Mrs. Wright wrote from Hollywood:

A HULL HOTEL
Hollywood Roosevelt
HOME OF THE STARS
HOLLYWOOD — CALIFORNIA

Dear Mrs. Hama,

The gods were kind to us — the weather is wonderful here — we were met with the smile of the sun.

It was so nice to have you been with you again — as usual it was refreshing to contact again your warmth and kindness. Your children are lonely — you did rarely well with them.

Your life is a constructive one and I was happy to see it.

As for myself — I am afraid — I was not at my best — the anxiety over Mr. Wright has been a great deal out of me. It seems every time I see you I say the same — Last year I was ill — this year I still carried with me the impression of Mr. Wright's illness. But life is a perpetual turning of the wheel and I happen to see you this past two years when it was turning at the bottom.

Please give my regards to Mr. Hama and all the best wishes for you

Olgivanna Lloyd Wright

P.S.
I wonder if there has been a package for me from N.Y.? If so won't you kindly send it to Lloyd Wright's address and they will mail it to me.

"See America First"

We agreed early with Mr. Wright that our house required plate glass. A lengthy strike in the glass industry had depleted the supply, so we started to explore glass purchase in January. Among those outlets contacted, one was especially encouraging, and on February 4 we wrote Mr. Wright:

We are enclosing an agreement for the plate glass. We will pay Mr. Kauffman of the Hotel Service Bureau a commission of five percent of this deal and inasmuch as he is receiving two percent reduction from the glass company it is really costing us only three percent commission.

Please check over the suggested form of order to see if it sufficiently protects us and return it airmail immediately inasmuch as they will hold this glass for us only until Monday or Tuesday of next week. We think we are extremely lucky to get it for it's a rare article on the coast.

The bulk of the glass was received in good condition soon after the order was placed. Later, when the sash arrived, we found that some panes were not cut exactly to our specifications. Fortunately, a detailed order form prepared by Mr. Kauffman protected us, and the faulty panes were replaced.

Originally Mr. Wright planned a large fireplace in the living room and a second, smaller one in the study. At length we decided to economize and forego the second fireplace for a decade; but we knew that eventually a library fireplace would have to be built; and we planned a foundation for it while the logistics were favorable.

John Scott, brick contractor, was employed by Mr. Turner on March 29 for a contract price of $1,400. Scott ordered wire-cut common San Jose brick and cement and sand from local suppliers and had them delivered to the site.

By the middle of May, Scott had been advanced $1,177.20 of the contract price and about three quarters of the brick pier and fireplace work had been finished. The quality of workmanship deteriorated and late in May the work stopped entirely. Scott and his crew did not show up. Suppliers informed Turner that Scott had not paid for materials. Turner wrote to Scott:

I am mailing this as a registered letter to make sure that you receive this notice. Since you have neglected to answer my letter of May 31 and have made no personal appearance on the job, I am hereby giving you three days to let me know whether you intend to complete your contract or not do any more about it.

If I don't hear from you, I will take it for granted that you have thrown up the job, and I will feel at liberty to use the balance of your contract money to complete your job. You have a little over $200 left, and I am sure that it will take all of that to complete your job in a presentable manner. The unpaid material bills you have are of course your responsibility, and you must take care of them.

I am mailing a copy of this letter to Mr. Albert Kelly, the California State Inspector of Contractors, to advise him of the position we are in, and also a copy to your material dealers, Rhodes and Robinson.

Scott evidently had gone on a long vacation. We employed a new crew of masons, tore down some unacceptable brickwork Scott did during his last week on the job, and completed the chimney. In addition to paying the new crew, we finally had to pay the materials supplier. It was most unfortunate that neither the Hannas nor Turner followed Mr. Wright's instructions to "pay no bills without approval from the architect."

The horizontal spine of our house was the invisible underground tunnel for utilities. A concrete floor and two sides of the tunnel had been poured and the forms removed. Irrigation water lines, drinking water lines, sewer pipes, and electrical conduits were installed in the tunnel. Pipes and conduits must rise through the concrete mat exactly into the space between both surfaces of a wooden wall; this demanded precise measurements before concrete could be poured. Similar precision was required for the placement of hot and cold air ducts within the walls. The conduits, pipes, and ducts were finally in place, stubbed above the level of the floor mat, and rigidly staked. Then gravel was laid four inches thick over the entire area where the concrete mat was to extend. Also at this time, a concrete cover was poured over the eighty-foot-long utilities tunnel and over the furnace room.

The mat itself, the floor of the house and terraces, consisted of two layers of reinforced concrete, each approximately three inches thick. The lower mat was divided into several pouring segments, separated from each other to reduce the possibility of cracks continuing from segment to segment. Steel reinforcing bars and heavy wire mesh were laid and staked over the gravel base. All concrete had to be mixed on the job in a small gasoline-powered cement mixer. Pouring the segments of the bottom three-inch layer of the mat took several days.

When the under layer of concrete segments was cured, we were ready to start the more exacting task of pouring and finishing the upper layer of floors and terraces. Building paper was placed over the earlier pour to separate the lower and upper layers of the slab. Again, heavy reinforcing wire mesh and bars were used to strengthen the concrete top layer. To avoid the transfer of stresses from the bottom pour to the upper layer, the edges of the pouring segments were offset from one layer to the next.

While the top layer was still soft, a mixture of red oxide and lamp black was worked into the surface to give a rich brick color. Most exacting care was required in marking the hexagon pattern on the freshly poured mat. Chalk lines were snapped into the soft concrete in three directions. Where walls, exterior and interior, were to be placed on these unit lines, metal strips were embedded in the concrete. These strips (brass was called for but we settled for zinc) were 1.5 inches high by 0.475 of an inch thick and cut as long as the walls to be set over them. We pressed the strip 0.75 of an inch into the soft concrete. This left 0.75 of an inch of metal above the finished surface of the mat. The studs and the sash were rabbeted at the bottom, treated with preservative, filled with mastic, and set on the protruding metal strips. At exterior walls, the strips would prevent surface water from passing into the interior of the building and, at the same time, hold the studs and sash rigidly in place. This construction (rather than nailing a wood sill into the concrete) prevented side-slipping of a wall.

When the metal strips were in place, a tool was used to complete the marking of the hexagons. When the six sides of a unit were tooled, the remaining chalk marks were eliminated by troweling.

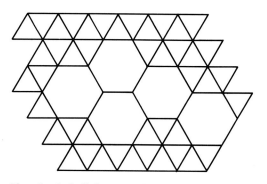

Sketch of chalk-line marks in fresh concrete mat

This is a good place to illustrate the unpredictable mistakes we sometimes made with this hexagonal grid system. In order to mark the unit lines in the first segments of the top layer of the mat, we made the following calculations:

Each side of the hexagon is two units in length. The unit measurement is 13 inches. Two units would be 26 inches. The distance between opposite points of a hexagon is twice the distance of one of the sides, 2 times 26 inches or 52 inches. One quarter of the distance between opposite points would be $\frac{1}{4}$ of 52 inches or 13 inches.

Knowing the measurements of two sides of a right-angle triangle (B and C), we can obtain the length of the third side.

$$A^2 = C^2 - B^2$$
$$A^2 = 26''^2 - 13''^2$$
$$A = 22.5''$$

Therefore, the perpendicular distance between parallel sides of a hexagon is 2 times 22.5 inches or 45 inches. This 45-inch figure was used to establish the

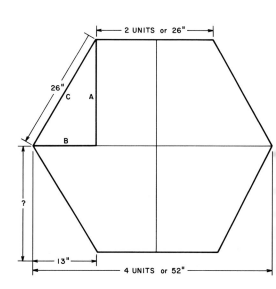

position of the nails as anchors for snapping the chalk lines.

On the day the crew was pouring and finishing the first small segment of the top mat, Paul was conducting a graduate seminar at the university. His secretary entered the room and asked him to go immediately to the site. There he found the foreman and crew in a deep quandry. They had poured and marked a segment ten tiles wide, and the overall distance was in error by 0.33 of an inch. If they continued to mark tiles this way they would compound a small error into a critical mismatch at the end of the house. Approximately 100 hexagon tiles were to be marked in the long axis of the mat for house and terrace; the compounded error would be about 3 inches. Paul suspected the 45-inch measurement must be in error. Consequently the formula for finding the measurement of one unknown side of a right angle triangle was carried out to eight decimal places; the correct measurement was 2 times 26.516666 inches or 45.0333321 inches. This .03-inch error in one tile would accumulate to .3-inch in 10 tiles or about 3 inches in 100 tiles.

Had this error not been detected before the first pour had hardened, the precut boards, battens, sash, and jambs would have been short at the far end of the building, and the metal strips, electrical conduits, and air ducts would have been placed incorrectly in the concrete mat.

The foundations were in; the cement floor slab was being poured. People by the score tramped up the hill, wandered amid the construction debris, and tried to make sense out of the "weird" shapes. Some came to molest. This necessitated hiring a young man to monitor the site when workmen, superintendent, or owners were not present. We thought this a happy solution until a colleague phoned and said, "We wondered how you planned to pay for this house. Now we know." When we asked for specifics, our friend said, "Shame on you, charging a fee of people interested enough to go up and have a look at what you are doing up there." This stunned us. We promptly went to the site and discovered that our enterprising watchman was charging twenty-five cents a person for a tour complete with a discarded scrap of copper roofing. We caught him in the act. As the sightseers departed, we asked our budding entrepreneur to return the money. We were embarrassed, but perhaps our watchman felt that tour-conducting was above and beyond guard duty and should be compensated appropriately.

What was the public's reaction to this strange construction? Everything

Laying reinforcing wire mesh before pouring top mat

Two sections of 3-inch top mat ready to be poured over 3-inch under mat

Pressing the 1½-inch metal strips into scored lines where walls will be erected

63

conceivable was criticized, from the Hannas' temerity in ruining a beautiful hill to their building such a "monstrosity." One of our most cherished stories came from the president of the university. He was visited by two very senior faculty men. They said, "Dr. Wilbur, are you aware that you have a madman on your faculty?"

"Why no," responded the president. "Tell me about it."

"Dr. Wilbur, he's a new young faculty member building an atrocious house over on Frenchman's Hill; only a madman would consider putting up such an outrageous structure. It's our recommendation that you get rid of him before tenure comes up."

The answer, verbatim, was, "Tell me, gentlemen, when do you plan to move into this house?"

Silence.

"Well then, gentlemen, if you don't plan to live there, I don't believe I'd worry about it."

Case dismissed. Most visitors who came to scoff remained to praise.

———————————————

During April, May, June, and July, the construction moved forward haltingly. Almost daily we faced unexpected problems. We asked for specifications with which to proceed:

Sanctum fireplace and chimney (telegram of April 5 and letter of April 14)
Manufacture and strengthening of flitch plate (letter of April 14)
Cabinetwork and furniture (telegram of May 8)
Sash and doors (telegram of May 8)
Screens between kitchen and living room and playroom (telegram of May 8)
Details for sash and furniture (telegram of May 25)
Hardware—hinges and locks (letter of May 27)
Door sheaves and track for playroom glass wall (letter of June 16)
Landscaping (letter of June 23)
Flower boxes (letter of June 23)
Cabinet details (telegram of July 14)
Doors to terrrace from playroom and living room (telegrams of July 14, 29)
Fence (telegram of July 29)

Mr. Wright answered some of our requests promptly with sufficient detail for us to proceed. To illustrate: we had local engineering advice that the flitch plates as designed would not carry the roof load without sagging. Mr. Wright on April 25 sent us a handwritten note with a sketch of a clever method of adding strength to this bearing member (see opposite page). In this instance we had not been able to delay the placing of the flitch plate

Dear Paul —   4-25-37

The overhead member you mention in your telegram was to have been — 2 – 2×10 S with 1/4" × 10" flitch plate continuous end to end (spliced if necessary) and about 40 feet long.

The actual span is about 24'-0 where the fixed sash are in place supporting the overhead member. If this proves insufficient — truss the flitch with heavy telephone wire, one wire each side of 2×10's, — Thus

wire → ← wire
pipe.

1¾ pipe let into 2×10 each side wound and soldered.

2×10

1¾ pipe

13/4 pipe

1¾ pipe

24'0

(crown 3/4" at center)

Sash

Sash

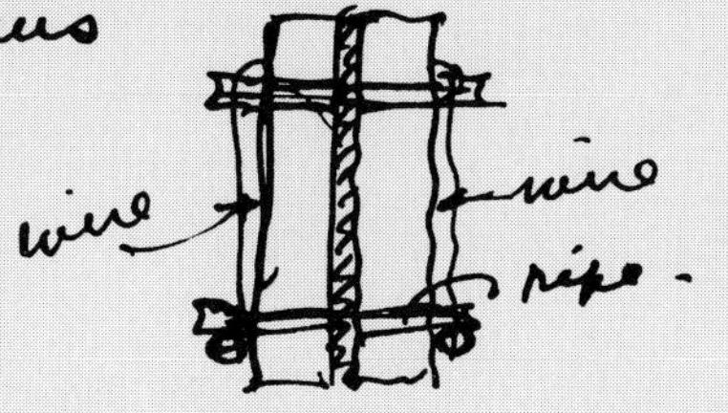

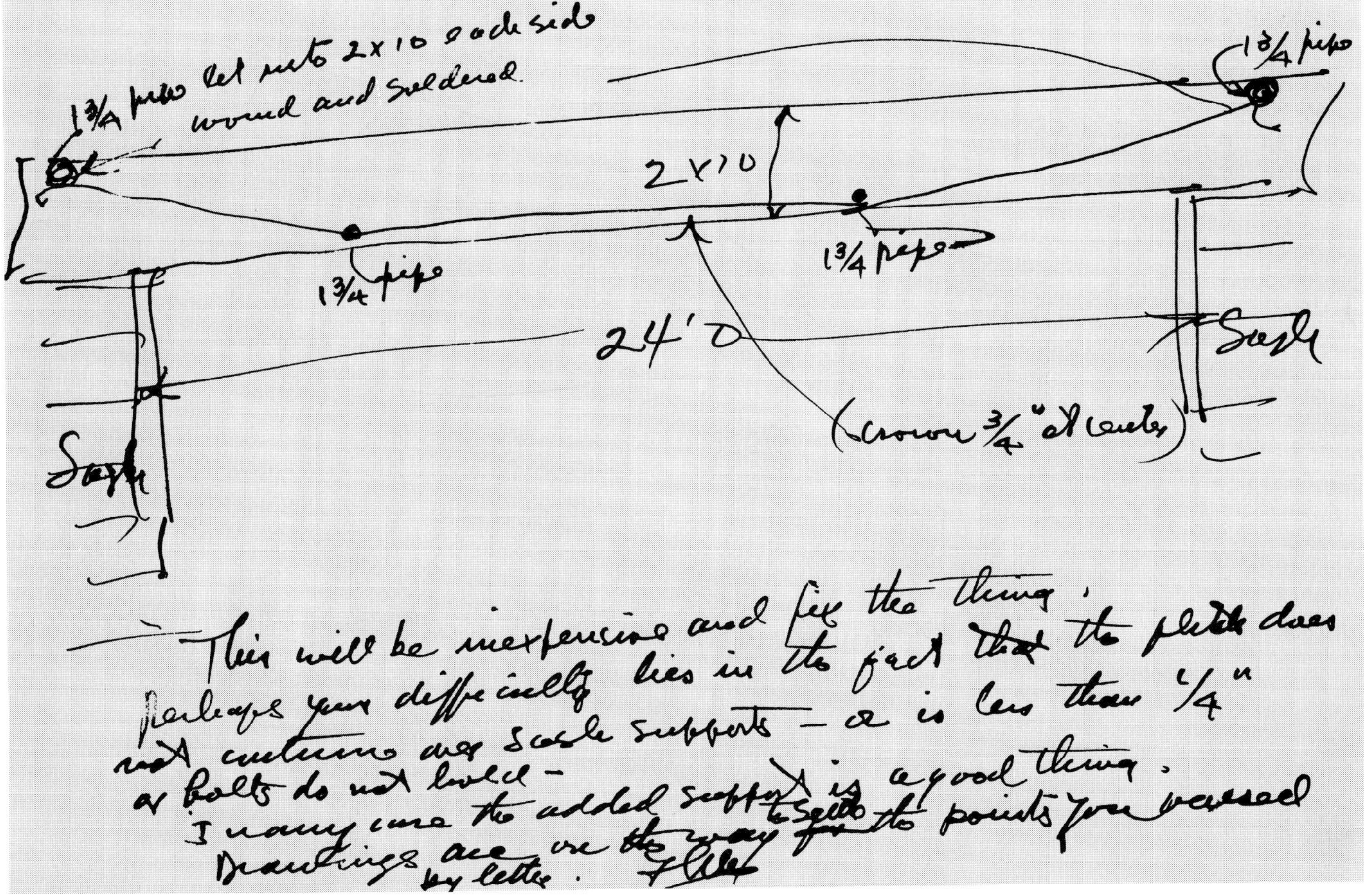

This will be inexpensive and fix the thing. Perhaps your difficulty lies in the fact that the flitch does not continue over sash supports — or is less than 1/4" or bolts do not hold —

In any case the added support is a good thing. Drawings are on the way to points you passed by letter. — Fleet until we heard from Mr. Wright, so we could not use his solution when it arrived. Inasmuch as there has not been noticeable sagging over the years, we evidently did not need any added strength.

On August 4, in exasperation and with a lack of good manners, we telegraphed Mr. Wright as follows:

FOR HEAVEN'S SAKE SEND NECESSARY DETAILS. SEND AIRMAIL COMPLETED DETAILS OF BEDS AND WARDROBES WHICH I SAW TALIESIN EARLY JUNE AWAITING YOUR APPROVAL. GAVE JACK LIST OF NEEDED DETAILS THEN, AND WE HAVE RECEIVED NOTHING. DELAYS ARE COSTLY IN TIME AND MONEY.

On August 6 we received the following telegram from Mr. Wright:

ALL LEFT TUESDAY MORNING SPECIAL DELIVERY. GET SQUARE WITH LAO-TSE.*

Drawings did arrive as promised in the August 6 mail. We had them blueprinted and promptly returned the originals and one set of prints to Taliesin.

As always, our reaction to the beauty of the new designs overcame any negative thoughts and feelings held before we unrolled the drawings. The evidence was in the designs. Mr. Wright and the apprentices had been busy creating better and better solutions. What more could one ask than solutions which surpassed earlier expectations?

Soon after receiving the roll of plans, we had a letter from Jack Howe, one of Mr. Wright's chief assistants.

In answer to your sheet of questions and requests:

. . . For the double deck beds the upper bed is identical with the lower bed bolted securely to the walls, the bottom of the frame 3 feet 3 inches above the lower bed (that is, at the fifth redwood board from the floor). No other supports for the upper bed are needed. A simple ladder of redwood should be built between the two beds (see detail).

We will send drawings for the easy chairs (six in the living room), straight chairs, and hassocks as soon as possible; also the fireplace crane and irons.

The laboratory floors should be covered with linotile the same color (goldenrod) as the carpets (see sample).

In the playroom we will have stools and hassocks; in the entry no chairs; in the sanctum two easy chairs, two straight; two easy, two straight in the master's bedroom; one easy chair, one straight in each of the other bedrooms.

We will send drawings for the pool, entrance feature, cave entrance, redwood fence, and barbecue fireplace as soon as Mr. Wright designs them.†

* Lao-Tse said, 2,500 years ago, that the present was "the ever-moving infinite that divides yesterday from tomorrow."

† The detail of the ladder and the carpet sample were not included in the reply. The cave-entrance plan was abandoned.

Central chimney under construction

Carport rafters hung from flitch plates

Bathtubs set in roof of utilities tunnel

Masonry completed, the roof construction is started

Brick front with roof completed, before delivery of window sash

In early August we mailed a photograph of the completed copper roof to Mr. Wright. He telegraphed on August 10 that something had gone wrong with the roof. We had reached the limit of our patience. We sent off a bitter letter to Mr. Wright on August 15.

We received your telegram Thursday. . . . We are at a loss to know what is wrong with the roof. We thought that it was one of the more satisfactory jobs which have been done. No doubt you see in the photos something that is radically wrong. But not knowing anything about copper roofs or architecture, we had to rely on a combination of Turner's judgment and the technical knowledge of the roofing people concerning the nature and application of their material. As far as we know, the roof is on just as you specified. We do not have a blueprint and specifications of the copper roof—you sent those plans directly to the copper roof company without sending us a copy. If you tell us what you believe is wrong, we will try to trace the process to see where errors have been made.*

All of this brings us to state a grievance which we feel must be aired at this time.

You assured us that this house could not cost us over $25,000. You will remember that we had estimated that it would cost a minimum of $34,000. You said this was absurd. We believed you. And now that the construction is nearly completed, the costs have run to over $37,000 . . . we have to pay our bills. We are going to be heavily in debt for the next twenty years. Well, the events are irrevocable, and we are glad that we have the house but you should know at what a price this has been achieved. When you come, you can say where we have made errors.

Your telegram stated that you wanted no bills paid until you passed on the details. The copper was finished six weeks ago. We paid in full at that time. Because of your inability to travel to Stanford, we assumed we had to pay the bills even though you had not passed on the work. We could not withhold payment indefinitely. You had not said before your last telegram that you might come out again. We asked you in two letters about your coming out and twice we spoke of it to you and the boys. Never did we receive from you the particulars about whose responsibility it was, in your absence, to pass on completion of subcontracts.

We will hold payment on all unpaid bills until you come next week.

This letter is written partially to prepare you for disappointments that must be yours when you arrive. But arrive you will and the sooner the better for all of us. We are as proud of our home as it is possible for humans to be—we mean proud in the real sense. And WE and YOU will be better pleased if you come out *now* while there is still time to correct some of the things that we are sure you can improve. In six more weeks we will be living in the new home. Unless you and the balance of the plans arrive within the week, we will be living in the midst of unfinished confusion for some time to come.

(Opposite page) Section through living room, above

Section through living room, laboratory, bathroom, and bedroom, below

* We discovered several years later what had gone wrong with the copper roof. When we were contemplating adding the wing, William Wesley Peters, of the Taliesin Associated Architects, sent us a roofing plan in which the pattern of ridges of copper run parallel with the roof hip and the eaves. In 1937 the copper subcontractor followed the pattern of the rafters underneath. He did not show us the plan Mr. Wright had sent only to him. Either the subcontractor had substituted a plan of his own, or Turner decided that the ridges should follow the rafter pattern. When the present Haydite roofing is replaced, it is our hope that copper can be used and the ridges be made to run the proper way.

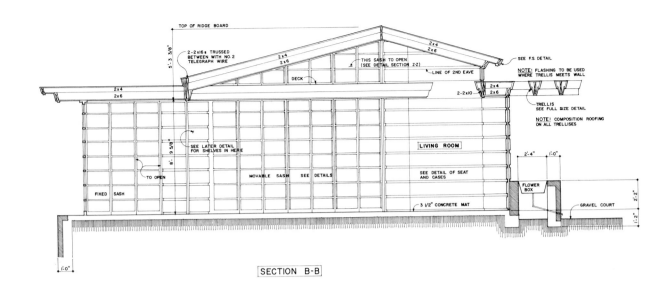

TOP OF RIDGE BOARD

2-2x16 s TRUSSED
BETWEEN WITH NO.2
TELEGRAPH WIRE

5'- 3 3/8"

2x4
2x6

2x4
2x6

DECK

THIS SASH TO OPEN
(SEE DETAIL SECTION Z-Z)

LINE OF 2ND EAVE

SEE F.S. DETAIL

NOTE: FLASHING TO BE USED
WHERE TRELLIS MEETS WALL

2-2x10
2x4
2x6

TRELLIS
SEE FULL SIZE DETAIL

NOTE: COMPOSITION ROOFING
ON ALL TRELLISES

LIVING ROOM

SEE LATER DETAIL
FOR SHELVES IN HERE

8'- 9 5/8"

TO OPEN

MOVABLE SASH   SEE DETAILS

SEE DETAIL OF SEAT
AND CASES

2'- 4"   1'-0"

FIXED SASH

FLOWER
BOX

3 1/2" CONCRETE MAT

GRAVEL COURT

2'-2"

1'-2"

1'-0"

SECTION B-B

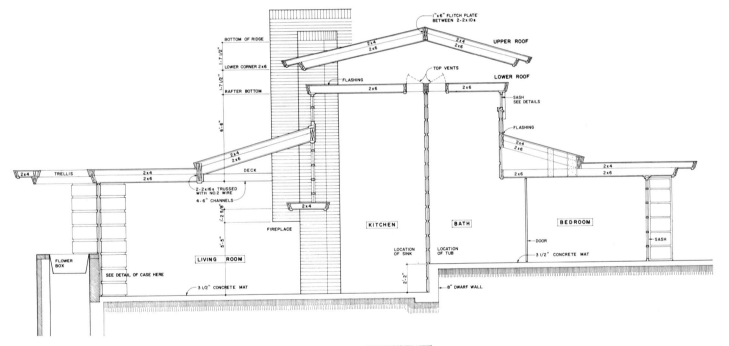

BOTTOM OF RIDGE

1'-7 1/2"

LOWER CORNER 2x6

1'-7 1/2"

RAFTER BOTTOM

1"x6" FLITCH PLATE
BETWEEN 2-2x10 s

2x4
2x6

UPPER ROOF

FLASHING

2x6

TOP VENTS

LOWER ROOF

2x6

SASH
SEE DETAILS

6'-6"

2x4
2x6

FLASHING

2x4
2x6

2x6

2x4
2x6

2x4
2x6

TRELLIS

2x4
2x6

DECK

2-2x16 s TRUSSED
WITH NO.2 WIRE

4-6" CHANNELS

1'-2 5/8"

2x4

KITCHEN

BATH

BEDROOM

SASH

FIREPLACE

LOCATION
OF SINK

LOCATION
OF TUB

DOOR

3 1/2" CONCRETE MAT

5'-5"

FLOWER
BOX

SEE DETAIL OF CASE HERE

LIVING ROOM

3 1/2" CONCRETE MAT

2'-2"

8" DWARF WALL

SECTION A-A

Mr. Wright's reply was prompt and direct. He wrote us on August 18 as follows:

(Opposite page) Section of details of walls and ceilings

I have read your letter of August 15 with mixed feelings. For one thing, I am sorry to have lost the benefit that would have come to the architect if the cost side of his work came right. We shall probably never build another house in Palo Alto. I cannot see how you got in this far without knowing where you were and letting me know.

You know I would not have let the thing go on at all if I hadn't seen in you a more than ordinarily capable client and in Turner a good builder whose judgment I had no reason to doubt, and after visiting the job, good reason to respect. I upped his figures before I would let you start. I let your contract with him stand after seeing his work and believing him all right.

I did take too much for granted, I see now. For instance it would never occur to me that any owner would settle with a contractor or subcontractor with no certification from his architect.

Alice Millard once did so and precipitated trouble but she was a business woman—she thought so anyway.

I am not able to say what ran the figures so far over the $30,000 limit I set including the guest house and the built-in furnishings.

I have nothing at all to go on to form an opinion.

As for the details, we did pretty well considering the break of my illness and the fact that we made you twice as many [drawings] as we ever made for any house before. It is true that the house is so highly a specialty that more superintendence should have been meted out to you but it would be so expensive at that distance that I didn't propose it because I thought everything was going well enough. I didn't want to increase the cost of the house unnecessarily.

Had I known what was happening, I should have insisted upon more expenditures for that item [superintendence] you may be sure. I think the best time for me to come now is when you are ready to move in—so that I can help you settle.

We have now sent you everything you asked for in detail except the fence and that goes off with this.

The only consolation I can offer you for being in debt—like me—is that it is a spur to action and that unlike most home owners you have something worthwhile to show for the "indebtedness."

However that doesn't satisfy me.

I feel badly about the whole business and almost wish we hadn't gone on with it.

My best to you both.

We might have attempted to reply to the logic and the specifics of Mr. Wright's letter. But what would have been gained by carrying on this exchange? Little, if anything. Consequently we relaxed and waited.

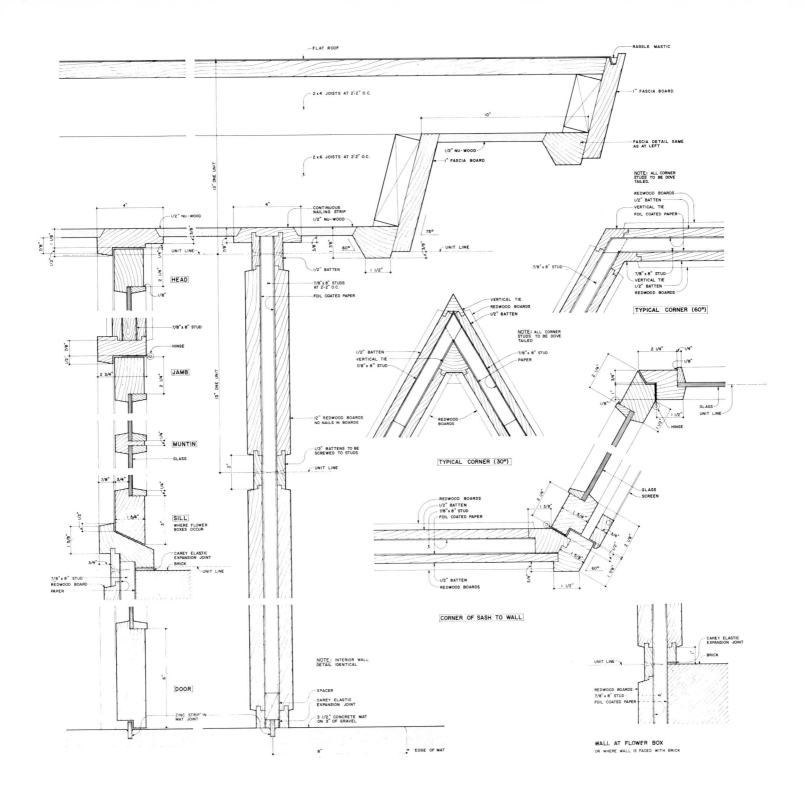

FLAT ROOF

RAGGLE MASTIC

2 x 4 JOISTS AT 2'-2" O.C.

1" FASCIA BOARD

10"

1/2" NU-WOOD

1" FASCIA BOARD

FASCIA DETAIL SAME AS AT LEFT

2 x 6 JOISTS AT 2'-2" O.C.

NOTE: ALL CORNER STUDS TO BE DOVE TAILED.

REDWOOD BOARDS
1/2" BATTEN
VERTICAL TIE
FOIL COATED PAPER

7/8" x 8" STUD

CONTINUOUS NAILING STRIP

1/2" NU-WOOD

1/2" NU-WOOD

75°

UNIT LINE

60°

UNIT LINE

7/8" x 8" STUD
VERTICAL TIE
1/2" BATTEN
REDWOOD BOARDS

TYPICAL CORNER (60°)

HEAD

1/2" BATTEN

7/8" x 8" STUDS AT 2-2" O.C.

FOIL COATED PAPER

7/8" x 8" STUD

HINGE

VERTICAL TIE
REDWOOD BOARDS
1/2" BATTEN

JAMB

NOTE: ALL CORNER STUDS TO BE DOVE TAILED.

1/2" BATTEN
VERTICAL TIE
7/8" x 8" STUD

7/8" x 8" STUD
PAPER

2 1/4"

1/4"

1/8"

MUNTIN

GLASS

12" REDWOOD BOARDS NO NAILS IN BOARDS

REDWOOD BOARDS

GLASS

UNIT LINE

HINGE

SILL
WHERE FLOWER BOXES OCCUR

1/2" BATTENS TO BE SCREWED TO STUDS

UNIT LINE

TYPICAL CORNER (30°)

GLASS SCREEN

CAREY ELASTIC EXPANSION JOINT

BRICK

7/8" x 8" STUD
REDWOOD BOARD
PAPER

UNIT LINE

REDWOOD BOARDS
1/2" BATTEN
7/8" x 8" STUD
FOIL COATED PAPER

60°

1/2" BATTEN
REDWOOD BOARDS

CORNER OF SASH TO WALL

NOTE: INTERIOR WALL DETAIL IDENTICAL

CAREY ELASTIC EXPANSION JOINT

BRICK

DOOR

SPACER

CAREY ELASTIC EXPANSION JOINT

3 1/2" CONCRETE MAT ON 3" OF GRAVEL

UNIT LINE

REDWOOD BOARDS
7/8" x 8" STUD
FOIL COATED PAPER

ZINC STRIP IN MAT JOINT

8"

EDGE OF MAT

WALL AT FLOWER BOX
OR WHERE WALL IS FACED WITH BRICK

On August 23 we wrote the following letter to Mr. Wright:

(Opposite page) Details of jambs

Today we received a roll of detailed plans which make us glow with satisfaction. The fireplace iron crane is a lovely thing. . . . The fence will be beautiful.

We are sorry you think you will wait until late in September to come west. We move in the last week of that month.* We will need you to help us get settled.

The following bills have not been paid or have been only partially paid:

Plumbing	¼ Paid	Road Surfacing	Not Paid
Heating	¹⁄₁₀ Paid	Electrical	¾ Paid
Nu-wood	Not Paid	Concrete Labor	¼ Paid
Mill Sash	Not Paid	Glazing	Not Paid
Mill Doors	Not Paid	Hardware	Not Paid

Shall we refuse to pay anymore until you arrive and pass on the work? In that case when may I say you are expected?

We, of course, pay our carpenter and general labor each week.

Please forgive our childish wailing from time to time. You know that we love this house regardless of the delays and financial sacrifices. It is the loveliest shelter we have ever seen. . . . Somehow, we will pay for it with the conviction that it is worth every frustration and sacrifice.

We do question whether you are fully conscious of the terrific cost for carpenters and other crafts to work the 120 degree angle. When you come we will show you some of the difficulties which ran up the costs unavoidably.

One illustration. We figured it would take 7,000 square feet of Nu-wood to cover ceilings and take $600 for our own carpenter labor to do the job. We called in the Nu-wood people who make a business of applying their product and they said 6,000 square feet of material would be ample. They would do it for $300 and make a profit. We didn't argue but told them to proceed. The unusual angles wasted 25 percent of the material (used 8,000 square feet) and took over $400 in labor for the company to apply it. They lost $100 in wages with the two best workmen in their crew, plus the rent of tools and the overhead. [We helped to recover the loss.] Almost every job has ballooned in cost in a similar manner.

Turner and the mill people have insisted that shelves . . . should be solid redwood and not plywood. They are going ahead with *solid* wood. What do you say and why?

We are enclosing a few sheets which we hope you will use in communicating your answers on a number of points.

Please come out. We want you to check on items but mostly we want you to see the home which we believe crowns the work of the master.

———

We had to postpone our move until much later.

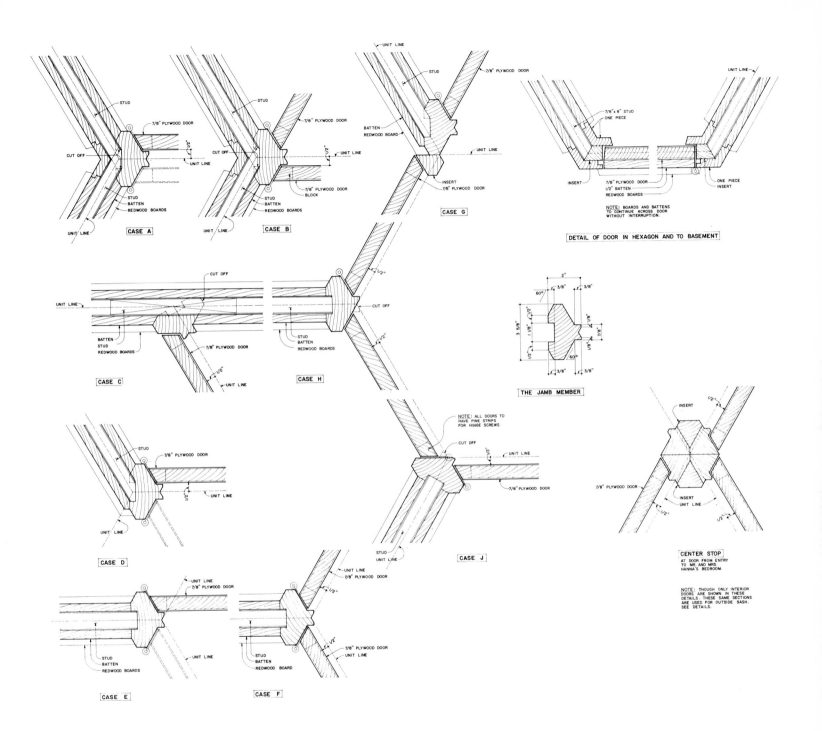

STUD
7/8" PLYWOOD DOOR
CUT OFF
1/2"
UNIT LINE
STUD
BATTEN
REDWOOD BOARDS
UNIT LINE
CASE A

STUD
7/8" PLYWOOD DOOR
CUT OFF
1/2"
UNIT LINE
7/8" PLYWOOD DOOR
BLOCK
STUD
BATTEN
REDWOOD BOARDS
UNIT LINE
CASE B

UNIT LINE
STUD
7/8" PLYWOOD DOOR
BATTEN
REDWOOD BOARD
UNIT LINE
INSERT
7/8" PLYWOOD DOOR
REDWOOD BOARDS
CASE G

UNIT LINE
7/8" x 8" STUD
ONE PIECE
7/8" PLYWOOD DOOR
UNIT LINE
7/8" x 8" STUD
ONE PIECE
INSERT
INSERT
7/8" PLYWOOD DOOR
1/2" BATTEN
REDWOOD BOARDS

NOTE: BOARDS AND BATTENS
TO CONTINUE ACROSS DOOR
WITHOUT INTERRUPTION.

DETAIL OF DOOR IN HEXAGON AND TO BASEMENT

CUT OFF
UNIT LINE
BATTEN
STUD
REDWOOD BOARDS
7/8" PLYWOOD DOOR
1/2"
UNIT LINE
CASE C

CUT OFF
STUD
BATTEN
REDWOOD BOARDS
1/2"
CASE H

2"
3/8" 3/8"
60°
1/2"
3 5/8"
1/8"
7/8"
1/8"
1/2"
60°
3/8" 3/8"

THE JAMB MEMBER

STUD
7/8" PLYWOOD DOOR
1/2"
UNIT LINE
UNIT LINE
CASE D

NOTE: ALL DOORS TO
HAVE PINE STRIPS
FOR HINGE SCREWS.
CUT OFF
1/2"
UNIT LINE
7/8" PLYWOOD DOOR
STUD
UNIT LINE
CASE J

INSERT
1/2"
7/8" PLYWOOD DOOR
INSERT
UNIT LINE
1/2"
CENTER STOP
AT DOOR FROM ENTRY
TO MR. AND MRS.
HANNA'S BEDROOM.

NOTE: THOUGH ONLY INTERIOR
DOORS ARE SHOWN IN THESE
DETAILS, THESE SAME SECTIONS
ARE USED FOR OUTSIDE SASH.
SEE DETAILS.

UNIT LINE
7/8" PLYWOOD DOOR
STUD
BATTEN
REDWOOD BOARDS
UNIT LINE
CASE E

UNIT LINE
7/8" PLYWOOD DOOR
1/2"
STUD
BATTEN
REDWOOD BOARD
7/8" PLYWOOD DOOR
UNIT LINE
1/2"
CASE F

On September 8, we wired Mr. Wright:

MOVING. NEED EASY CHAIRS STRAIGHT CHAIRS STOOLS. PLEASE RUSH DETAILS. WIRE WHETHER YOU WILL BE HERE TO APPROVE SUBCONTRACT.

Mr. Wright replied on October 1:

HAPPY DAYS. MAKE NO PAYMENTS. WILL WIRE ARRIVAL SOME TIME LATER.

On October 12, knowing of our upcoming trip, Mr. Wright wired:

NOT FEELING VERY WELL. ARRANGE TO STOP HERE WHEN YOU COME EAST AND I CAN GO OVER MATTERS IN DETAIL WITH YOU THEN. CAN SEE THE HOUSE WHEN WE GO TO ARIZONA SOMETIME AFTER THE FIF-TEENTH OF NOVEMBER.

Mr. Wright was able to visit us in November. From the Jokake Inn in Arizona, he wrote:

4 The light fixtures as corrected.

5 ~~The~~ Elimination of ^wood^ ~~knife edge~^strips^ in ledge of L.R and Playroom — changing direction of strips. I will gladly ~~pay~~ for the change in the living-room rather than ~~not~~ have it done.

6. The holes, ^for thrust bolts^ in shelf to keep the ~~wooden~~ ^kitchen^ blinds ~~at~~ the proper angle.

7 ~~Elimination of ~~outside~~ One~~ Shelf added above ~~the~~ cabinet by Dining table and one added below kitchen-blinds as explained to Tuma and yourself also the dish cabinet in the recess where the dining table is put, as explained if you can manage it.

8 Elimination of stage-lights around ^outside^ cornice.

9 Put louvres over glass in Outside ventilator Tuma has sketch.

All ~~little things~~ but very important in a finished performance ~~like this one~~.

We will make a detail of piano-screen and ~~halyard~~ ^as^ top and bottom to complete the new copper-lamp according to the grammar of Honeycomb.

Finally the admonition of the mysterious stranger — the man who corrupted Hadleyburg.} "Go and reform, ^for^ you are by no means a bad man"—Paak. Meaning your conscience. I thought I saw a little sense of guilt and worry for spending so much more than you intended. Never mind — you will have forgotten it five years hence and enjoy your economics ~~in~~ meantime. Affectionately to you all — you look so well in the ^bee^ cells that were made to imprison you in sunlight.

FLl.

During his visit, Mr. Wright passed on the work and materials of sub-contractors so that we were free to pay most of the outstanding bills.

Mr. Wright was as unhappy as we were that errors had occurred. These errors were due to a combination of factors:

Mr. Wright's delays in supplying detailed drawings and in responding promptly to requests for directions on specific problems;

Mr. Wright's physical inability to be present during construction to supervise the vast number of problems arising from this first use, in an entire building, of the 120-degree angle;

Mr. Turner's tendency to change materials or construction, without our architect's approval, when Turner thought he had a better idea. Turner did contribute valuable suggestions, but he must share the responsibility with the Hannas for making certain modifications that had to be corrected;

the failure of some subcontractors to cope with the complexity of the project;

our failure to comprehend fully Mr. Wright's basic concept of the hexagonal grid system and of organic architecture;

our lack of experience in building. We had to serve as final authority in disputes between subcontractors and Turner. We had to consider Turner's or subcontractors' notions of what would or would not meet the specifications and blueprints. The work could not always wait for instructions from Taliesin, and our guesses, interpretations, and decisions were untutored and at times faulty.

It would be erroneous, however, to conclude that almost everything went wrong. There were far more successes than failures. To illustrate:

The choice of Mr. Pyle as the excavator and cement superintendent was fortunate. His work was top quality.

The selection of the Pacific Manufacturing Company as the supplier of all redwood and the millwork on all boards, jambs, fenestrations, and doors proved to be completely satisfactory. The president of the mill personally selected the kiln-dried heart redwood for the entire job.

The Simmons Mattress Company made all the pads, mattresses, and cushions with the 120-degree angles and charged us at the rate for regular 90-degree angle work.

The heating, plumbing, and electrical work were done by excellent mechanics with quality materials.

The crew of carpenters finally chosen was a joy to work with and produced cabinet-quality products.

We were fortunate in our choice of a foreman. Without Harold Turner, our house might never have been built.

The complete list of positive aspects of building the Hanna House is extensive, and in spite of frustrations we were able to move into our new home in the late autumn. We lived in the midst of confusion as carpenters and tradesmen rushed to complete last-minute details.

Both of us, husband and wife, had worked along with the laborers and craftsmen on the job. We took part in every type of construction: we mixed concrete, laid brick, sawed redwood, screwed on battens, set plate glass, put on insulation, held pipe for plumbers, made light fixtures. We filled vertical joints in masonry, a job overlooked by bricklayers. The children aided in cleaning away waste materials and running errands. We worked ourselves into the house construction as a family.

Mr. Wright gave us a home that left an imprint on the lives of our children. They know the subtle but true relations of form and purpose, of site and dwelling. For them, beauty is a way of living rather than "pictures to hang on walls." Our home is a natural gathering place for friends, and nothing can bring more happiness.

The only true test of a theory is the way in which it works. We can say that for us our house met the acid test of family life. The deep satisfaction of feeling that our dream had come true far exceeded the remembered difficulties and disappointments. We faced the future with optimism and a profound admiration for and gratitude to Frank Lloyd Wright.

Here is Mr. Wright's summary of the Hanna House, written in 1937:

Dr. Paul Hanna of Stanford University has just moved into his house. . . . Here the thesis changes, not in content but in expression. Again we have a preliminary study of prefabrication—also made in humble native materials—principally redwood board partitions erected on a concrete mat cut into hexagonal tiles. Another experiment because I am convinced that a cross section of honeycomb has more fertility and flexibility where human movement is concerned than the square. The obtuse angle [120 degrees] is more suited to human "to and fro" than the right angle. That flow and movement is, in this design, a characteristic lending itself admirably to life, as life is to be lived in it. The hexagon has been conservatively treated—however, it is allowed to appear in plan only and in the furniture which literally rises from and befits the floor pattern of the concrete slab upon which the whole stands. . . . This model for prefabrication was built by hand, not employing shop methods for which the work was primarily designed. The result is necessarily more expensive than need be were construction to have that advantage.

But this thesis goes far enough to demonstrate the folly of imagining that a true and beautiful house must employ synthetics or steel to be "modern," or go to the factory to be economical. Glass? Yes, the modern house must use glass liberally. . . .

To me here is a new lead into a fascinating realm of form, although somewhat repressed on the side of dignity and repose, in this first expression of the idea. I find it easy to take a definite unit of any simple geometric pattern and by modern technologies suited to the purpose, adjusted to human scale, evolve not only fresh appearances but vital contributions to a livelier domesticity. This house goes very far in conservation of space. I hope to demonstrate that no factory can take the house to itself but may itself go to the house. In the hands of one well-versed in the design of patterns for living it may come out continually refreshed by imagination—from within. . . .

The new Reality of which I bespeak is in this house, with certain reservations needful at the moment. Appreciative clients not afraid they were going to be made ridiculous were essential to this experiment. Without such help as Paul Hanna and his wife, Jean, gave to this experiment with their lives, nothing could ever have really happened in this direction. [The] University would have had just another one of those things—nice things but nevertheless just "things." *

(Opposite page) The Hanna House seen from approach road. Below, the entrance court.

* *The Architectural Forum, January, 1938, page 68.*

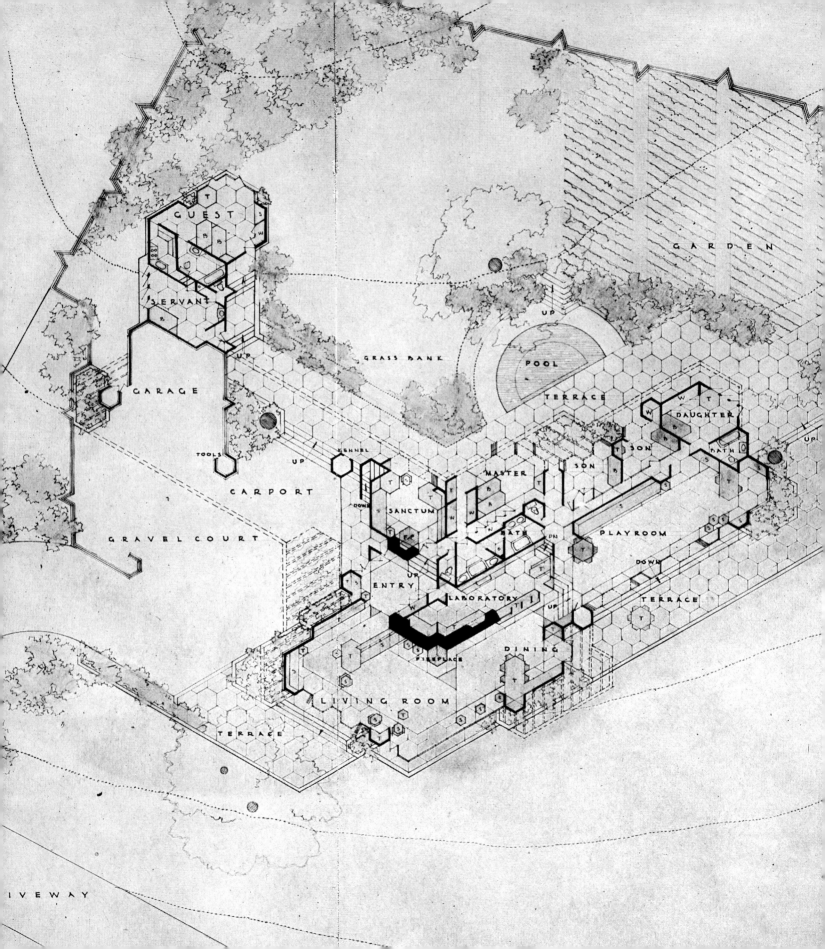

CHAPTER FOUR

Living and Learning

LATE in November, 1937, we left our rented dwelling in Palo Alto and moved to our new house at the edge of the Stanford campus. From a conventional two-story house on a small flat city lot, we moved into a one-story split-level home on an acre and a half of sloping terrain.

We entered the house through the foyer front doors. From the foyer, we could, at that first phase of construction, choose any one of three routes through the house: we might turn right and enter (no doors) the living room; we might move straight ahead through a single door into the kitchen in the center of the building; or we might turn to the left, mount four steps and enter the study (sanctum).

If we elected to go into the living room first, by easy turns we might travel leftward through this spacious room. Four easy steps led up into the playroom (again no doors). Continuing through the playroom we entered the daughter's bedroom at the east end of the house.

From the foyer, turning left up only four steps, we might enter the study. Passing through the study, we reached the master bedroom and bath area. Proceeding through the master bedroom, we could cross the service hall to find one son's bedroom. Or, taking the narrow hall serving only the children's bedrooms, we came first to another son's bedroom and, finally, at the east end of the house, again to the daughter's bedroom. Thus we could complete a traffic circle through all the major rooms of the house. The early floor plans and photographs taken in 1938 help to clarify the arrangement of interior space and traffic flow through the house.

As we moved into our home, old furniture was left behind, a break from our previous accoutrements. Old furnishings were sold or given away, but we kept our upright piano, Jean's cedar chest, and a child's rocking chair. Books, china, tools, kitchen supplies, clothing, and toys went with us.

Frames for beds and couches, wardrobes, dressers, book shelves, desks, and tables, designed by Mr. Wright, were built into the house. He designed

(Opposite page) Plan for the Hanna House, 1936

the dining room chairs, and we constructed eight of them in the temporary shop on the site. The Simmons Company delivered five sets of mattresses and springs as designed by Mr. Wright. Still to come as we moved in were six upholstered pads for built-in couches and benches. The beds in place, our bedding was adjusted easily to the unique head and foot angles. Dishes and cooking equipment were stowed properly; dishwasher, refrigerator, range, disposal unit, and other essential apparatus were in place. We were all happy and feeling like Hannas in Wonderland.

We were without floor coverings for a few weeks. Mr. Wright had designed carpets (goldenrod and blue) to conform to the hexagonal module. These carpets, produced by the Klearflax Company in Duluth, Minnesota, proved to be practical and aesthetically pleasing.

We consulted Mr. Wright on window shades. He advised us to avoid drapes and suggested Aeroshades. The Aeroshade, a product used by Mr. Wright in many of his houses, is made of thin horizontal hardwood slats. Ours were stained redwood color to match our walls. It was not long before the shades produced an unanticipated disagreement between the Hannas. Jean lowered the shades on the west wall of the living room during the afternoon, to protect fabrics and furniture from the sun's heat and light. Paul wanted to see the distant hills, the trees, and clouds. Therefore, he would raise the shades. This scenario was enacted for months until we finally resolved our difference by installing bronze plate glass outside the west windows of the living room. Thus we enjoyed our beautiful view without sun damage to the interior.

We were short of chairs in the living room for some time after we moved in. Still to come from a San Francisco cabinet shop were two large Wright-designed reading chairs, three hassocks, and three floor cushions.

Although we had moved into our house, there was considerable finishing to be done, and three of our cabinetmakers all but moved in with us. There were endless small details to be completed. Our youngsters loved the workmen and hoped they would stay indefinitely. However, the time finally arrived when we reluctantly told our carpenter friends that the cabinetwork was complete. Sadly, they packed up their tools. But, happily, they returned many times and brought their families to picnic with us and to admire their handiwork.

Most of the furniture was in place by late winter. Chairs and tables were built to our measure. Cupboards and shelves were plentiful.

The gas consumption for house heating was much less than that of our

Early views of living room

smaller rented house in Palo Alto. The insulation paper in the walls and the expanse of glass saved on winter heating bills.

The living room accommodated a hundred or more people without seeming crowded or noisy. Or two could sit alone in the evening by the fire and read, listen to music, or turn out the lights to look through glass walls to a star-studded sky or moonlit hills.

The playroom was dedicated to the children. On its floor might be a whole city made of toy blocks; on the shelves collections of rocks or shells; in the corner a rug being woven on the hand loom or a puzzle being cut out on the jigsaw. We built a puppet stage, and the children and their friends wrote and performed shows. Everyone was learning to use this new space.

During the next few months, we completed the interior of the house to the point where we felt we could invite the Wrights to visit.

On April 4, 1938, the Wrights and twenty apprentices arrived for the weekend. Mr. Wright had not seen the house since we settled in, and we were anxious about his reaction. As he stood in the living room and looked around, his first comment was, "Why, it's more beautiful than I had imagined; we have created a symphony here."

On Monday morning, Mr. Wright asked us to take him to Palo Alto, saying, "Our house cries out for *objets d'art*." We took him to The Homeware Store and watched with growing concern as Mr. Wright walked around, pointed to various items, and said, "We'll take that." As soon as we could slip into the back room, we said to our friend the owner of the store, "What are we going to do? We can't afford to buy all these items."

"No problem," said our friend. "Take them, and when Mr. Wright has gone home, bring them back." That is what we did, for the most part. Of course, there were items that seemed so right for the house that we bought them!

Frank Lloyd Wright in the Hanna House

As familiar as we were with the plans of Hanna House, there was adventure in adjusting to the reality of the new module. The two floor levels were just right: an illusion of two stories without all those stairs. The variation in ceiling heights from 6 feet 7 inches to 16 feet 3 inches delighted us. We enjoyed the openness of the plan and the free flow of space generated by the 120-degree angle.

Housework was easily organized. The kitchen, in the center of the house, provided an efficient work area. One did not feel shut away from family

The playroom

and friends there; it was possible to keep an eye on the children congregated in the playroom with their neighborhood friends. Tall hinged wooden fins separated the kitchen from both living room and playroom. These fins could be closed for formal entertaining and for privacy; otherwise they were open. The kitchen ceiling vents, when opened to the screened bonnet on the roof, kept cooking odors from pervading the house and acted as air-conditioning during the hot weather. An adjustment on the ventilating equipment allowed the furnace fans to circulate air throughout the house. Because this kitchen was so different from the standard, it proved of great interest to students who visited us. There was always one in a class who asked, "But, Mrs. Hanna, how can you work in a kitchen that doesn't have a window over the sink?" In response, Jean would point out the view of fields and Black Mountain through the open fins and the playroom glass walls.

Mr. Wright called the children's bedrooms "stalls." So they were. But a bed, wardrobe, desk, and chair sufficed, since there was the large playroom. The children were not unhappy, and the parents accepted their own tight quarters knowing these eventually would be altered.

The early controversy over the narrowness of the long hall between the youngsters' bedrooms and the playroom proved to be an exercise in triviality. This twenty-inch hall was in fact wide enough to walk through—even carrying a bed tray—and was a great conversation piece for guests during parties. On the occasion of our housewarming, one friend organized a game to see which corpulent guests could negotiate the entire length of the hall without turning sideways. Mr. Wright was correct: the hall was certainly adequate for its limited purpose.

Our youngsters loved to bring their friends to roam about the house; they were often puzzled by the angles and intrigued by the shapes of the beds. Many an evening, we had to extract a faculty child from an upper bunk and return him to his parents. The children and their playmates loved the playroom, where they ran the electric train, played records on an old wind-up Victrola, or painted at the easel. The uncarpeted floor was a good place for miniature croquet games. Later, the outgrown blocks and toys were supplanted by slumber parties and dances. At the end of the playroom was a cove the children called their study. It contained a built-in couch, table, bookshelves, and desk. It even served as a bedroom for René, a Bolivian student at Stanford, who lived with us for a year. (Later, as Bolivian consul-general to San Francisco, he returned to visit us.)

The master bedroom was large enough, but the dressing area was barely adequate. Beds in all four bedrooms were the occasion for many wantonly irreverent comments. As our correspondence with Mr. Wright shows, we had some misgivings about not only the width of the beds (thirty-three inches) but their angles, which, though they conformed to the hexagonal module, required custom-built springs and mattresses. We are indebted to the Simmons Mattress Company for their willingness to cope with the unusual. Their work held up well for twenty years.

Bath space was circumscribed; all three baths had sunken tubs. These tubs were not due, as suggested by some, to our penchant for the exotic; it

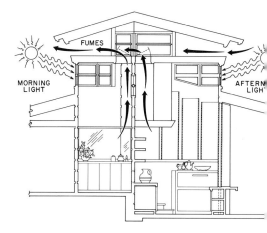

Section drawing showing light and ventilation

The laboratory, 1938

Original dining room table and chairs designed by Frank Lloyd Wright

was a matter of space. A sunken tub allows more body space in a small room.

The study was decidedly tight. We wonder how we ever managed. Two desks and a built-in couch left very little floor space. We did have shelves for research volumes, but most of our library books were in the living room. However, the study was restful and conducive to reading and writing.

The dining end of the living room was adequate for dinner parties of eight to ten persons. After some years we were able to convert the playroom to its planned ultimate function as dining room. Then the living room, with the dining function removed, could be at its best.

Mr. Wright often said, "Give me the luxuries and I'll get along without the necessities." We also indulged in the luxuries: art, textiles, books, and,

87

of course, music. Mr. Wright designed our house with music as a priority. A pianist and organist himself, he understood our desire to have an organ, but, always thinking big, he thought of a pipe organ. Although we preferred a pipe organ, we recognized that both the original cost and the upkeep were impossible for us. Nevertheless, we consented to Mr. Wright's including space for banks of organ pipes. We put off the organ decision for some years and contented ourselves with a small Baldwin upright. Finally the day came when we felt we had to have an organ. Our research led us to the Saville organ. When the designers came to Stanford and studied the acoustics of the house, they were delighted with the results. The lofts Mr. Wright had provided for pipes proved ideal for the installation of speakers. We installed 120 twelve-inch speakers throughout the house.

One new piece of equipment is likely to invite or require another. Our little Baldwin upright piano was no match for the Saville organ. So we purchased a Mason & Hamlin grand piano. This combination of instruments was most felicitous, and we and our friends enjoyed great music when Herbert Nanney, university organist, and Father John Olivier took turns on the two instruments. Occasionally President J. E. Wallace Sterling joined them.

We were particularly fond of chamber music. Both amateurs and such professionals as Adolph Geller (from Argentina) and our own Naomi Bonney and Adolph Baller favored us and our friends with evenings of music. Then there were those delightful jazz artists, Bill and Gertrude White, who brought their combo to our home and played jazz as it should be played.

The music area in living room, 1961

One delight of our house was the discovery of new ways to live and work within the house and on the terrace—of different places to eat, play, and relax. There were great views from almost every direction. This truly glass house has a minimum of opaque walls, and almost every room has access to a terrace through floor-to-ceiling glass doors.

The outside area of Hanna House was as usable as the inside. Large cement terraces provided a safe place for youngsters to master tricycles and skates. The ample grass lawn was suitable for croquet, archery, and badminton. Mr. Wright designed a small brick barbecue with concrete seats for enjoying the outside fireplace. The youngsters embedded in the seats mosaics from the earthquake-shattered university church.* The terraces and grassy yard served very well for picnics or wine and cheese parties. On occasion as many as two hundred students and faculty would participate in

---

* *At the time of the 1906 earthquake, the broken chunks of mosaic had been dumped in the dry lake bed below our hillside.*

A terrace, 1938

a pancake and fruit brunch.

The central location of the kitchen—with two pass-throughs and quick access through the service hall to the rest of the house and the terrace—made possible a choice of places in which to eat. After the 1957 remodeling we could breakfast in winter in front of the library fireplace or the fireplace in the master bedroom. In summertime, outdoor meals were favorites. While eating, we could watch quail, listen to doves and mockingbirds, and hear the splash of water in the fountain.

One thing we learned from Mr. Wright was the satisfaction of dissatisfaction; the virtue of continuous remodeling in favor of upgrading (with the architect's approval, of course). Jean was excellent at ripping out; Paul stressed reconstruction.

The first alteration was removing a built-in couch along the north wall of the living room; the couch space would. be better used for a record player and a shelf for record storage.

Other alterations included the beds in the master bedroom. While Mr. Wright was ill, one of the apprentices apparently had designed a seat with triangular tables for the foot of the beds. When Mr. Wright saw this, he declared it a physical hazard. Jean decided Mr. Wright was right and tore out the seat. Her destruction, which lengthened the beds six inches, left the mattresses six inches short. Paul noticed the gaps as well as the somewhat wobbly footboards. Jean then pieced out the mattresses with foam rubber and Paul properly finished the foot of the beds. The result was applauded by Mr. Wright the next time he visited.

The biggest reconstruction project involved the boys' bathroom. Jean did not like the laundry in the kitchen; it would be much more convenient in the boys' bathroom. If the washing machine came in, the tub had to go out. The tub was useless; the boys liked showers. How to make the change? Jean telephoned Mr. Wright for support. Not wanting to bother Paul, who was busy traveling to supervise government contracts for Stanford, Jean decided to undertake the job herself. The first task was to remove the tub, which was sunk in the utilities tunnel. What went in should certainly come out! The water and drain connections in the utilities tunnel were dismantled and then Jean, the older son, John, and the gardener managed somehow to hoist that bathtub out of the tunnel. No way would it go through the bathroom door! Jean had forgotten that the tubs were placed in the tunnel before the framing of the rooms. The gardener went back to his gardening. What to do? The solution involved removing the piano-hinged door and then the door frame. This worked, but the tub proved too heavy to carry. Finally, Jean and John were able to roll the tub out on pipe rollers and left it on the back terrace.

Jean tried to get university plumbers to make preparations for laundry equipment. No plumber was available; it was wartime, and the maintenance staff was depleted. Visits to two Palo Alto plumbing shops produced the same story. Jean then decided plumbing was something she had always wanted to do. She made measurements, bought equipment, and installed it herself. In thirty years it hasn't leaked!

The next job was to lay a concrete floor over the opening where the tub had been. This involved grinding out the concrete ledge where the tub had rested, building a wooden platform to support new concrete, laying metal reinforcing on the platform. Jean mixed concrete in a wheelbarrow. Unfortunately, the wheelbarrow, full of concrete, was too wide to push through the back door, so concrete had to be carried in buckets and dumped on the platform. Suppose the platform failed to hold? A lot of concrete would have fallen into the tunnel, burying all utilities! Fortunately, Jean had built better than she feared. After Paul returned, Jean found a new clothes washer and dryer in the bathroom where the tub had been—Paul's expression of satisfaction over a job well done.

Jean's daily presence at the original construction gave her the knowledge and courage to tackle such jobs. Indeed, the house seemed to invite all sorts of experiments. Our architect applauded these efforts to live imaginatively, and various makeover projects whetted our appetites for the planned next phase of the Hanna House.

The small study, that inviolate sanctum, had become virtually a family room. On any weekend, one might find parents working at their desks, one child drawing at the end of Daddy's desk, another playing with a pair of kittens, and the third generally disrupting everyone. In the evening, with the children in bed, the parents could at last concentrate on research and writing. The limited space heightened our eagerness to remake the interior of the main house to gain a library with more work room, more shelving, and more filing space. And we longed to read, write, and study with the warmth of a fireplace.

Two persistent questions arose: Are your house and your garden easy or hard to keep up? How much help do you have? The house was relatively easy to maintain; in the forty-some years we lived in the house, the walls were refinished (with wax-based varnish) once; the carpets replaced once.

91

The largest job was dusting, but the walls, shelves, and furniture of redwood made the dust less visible! The youngsters maintained their own rooms; this worked as well as might be expected. Occasionally we were tempted to weaken in enforcing this rule; for example, when son Robert found it expedient to clean and rearrange his bedroom on Saturday beginning at midnight. Each year the youngsters were given more complex tasks to encourage them to feel involved in a family enterprise.

Jean's household responsibilities were those of the typical faculty wife and mother, but her professional writing schedule necessitated a part-time maid to share housekeeping and child supervision.

Our 1½-acre plot soon demonstrated that a part-time gardener was essential; none of us was fully competent or had sufficient free time to cope with nature. Paul could have handled it, but his university commitments, government projects, and publishing contracts allowed very little time for garden chores. A one-day-a-week gardener-maintenance man sufficed to keep the yard and gardens fairly presentable, and on weekends the whole family would often put in frenzied hours getting the place in shape.

How much did maintenance cost at Hanna House? Understandably, people wanted to know what financial obligation was incurred in maintaining a house of this size and construction. At right is our estimate for 1965:

ESTIMATED COSTS, 1965	
County tax (house & grounds)	*$2,000*
Insurance (complete coverage)	*1,500*
Grounds:	
gardener, spraying, supplies	*2,000*
Window washing	
(4 times @ $65)	*260*
Heat and light	*740*
Maid service	*300*
Ground rent (including water)	
to Stanford	*100*
Repairs (plumbing, electrical,	
heating, paving)	*500*
Annual Total	*$7,400*

There was one problem the Hannas had not anticipated when they decided to build a house designed by Frank Lloyd Wright: the curiosity as well as genuine interest of the public. We were not really concerned that scores of people climbed our hill to inspect construction while we were building. As long as they didn't interfere with workmen or walk across fresh concrete, we pretty much ignored them. But after the family moved in, we couldn't believe the number of people appearing at the door, asking to go through the house. We couldn't tolerate total strangers peering through our glass walls and finally had to establish a rule: we would welcome house visitors only by appointment. (However, when people from foreign countries appeared at our door, we invariably admitted them.) We would not allow visitors to look around the outside of the house unaccompanied, a frequent request that, for obvious reasons, we could not honor. We were glad to spend (and usually did) an hour or more showing visitors our home and answering questions, provided they had made a proper appointment.

Professors Ray Faulkner and Victor Thompson (of the Art and Architecture Departments at Stanford) had our yearly invitation to hold classes and seminars in the Hanna House. Architectural classes came year after year from as far away as the states of Washington, Kansas, and Arizona. Classes from more than twenty colleges or universities visited us. Individual students came from most states and forty-eight nations. Every year a group of Japanese architects, members of the Frank Lloyd Wright Society of Japan, visited us under the direction of Professor and Mrs. Masami Tanigawa. Many long-lasting friendships resulted from these encounters.

We have albums of letters postmarked from every continent and most U.S. states, written by people who visited us over the years. Most expressed understanding as well as gratitude. Following is a facsimile of a letter from the Taliesin Fellowship.

DR.AND MRS.PAUL R.HANNA: CORONADO STREET: STANFORD UNIVERSITY: CALIFORNIA

Dear Dr.and Mrs.Hanna: All of us thank you for the delicious supper and pleasant evening last Sunday and for the restful day at your home on Monday. We only hope it was not too tiring for you to have the horde of us settle down on you.

The Fellowship anticipates with great pleasure another visit to the Hannas and we hope the Hannas will visit us both at Taliesin in Wisconsin and here in the desert.

Sincerely yours,

THE TALIESIN FELLOWSHIP
Spring Green, Wisconsin
Scottsdale, Arizona
April 11th, 1938

A Stanford undergraduate from Germany wrote:

At this point I am in my room at Toyon Hall still overwhelmed by your kindness and graciousness to share your home with myself and the others in Dr. [Victor] Thompson's class. Your home denotes all that a home should I think, and there are probably not enough superlatives for it. There is one word in German that would describe it but one can't really translate the meaning of this word, rather one must feel it in your heart, mind, and body. This is what your home conveys to me though, all the warmth and emotion, labor and love that I know so well can be put into a home such as yours.

Needless to say, I am not only now a "fan" of Mr. Wright but also one of you and your husband and the effort that you put forth. I just can't say enough in appreciation and gratitude, but then maybe I have already said too much.

A professor of architecture from another university sent this message:

I should like to convey the sincere thanks of our fifth-year students and their professors who recently were so kindly welcomed into your home. For many it was a first experience inside a house designed by Frank Lloyd Wright. For me, it was the first where Mr. Wright had worked closely with the owners. I have never before sensed so strong a unity of site, client, and architecture.

It was a truly rewarding experience. . . .

A weekend visitor, architecturally poetic, wrote:

Rarely in houses of modern times do I feel on easy terms with my surroundings. I was surprised to find myself so emotionally familiar with the place, a wonderfully secluded shelter, with the kind of aura I knew in the big old houses of my childhood. But no house of my childhood was ever so casually joined with the outdoors, so profusely fenestrated and skylighted, or so varied in levels and ceiling heights. I particularly enjoyed the feeling of space to move around in and somewhere to go. The angled partitions don't cut you off; they lead you on—much as the carefully placed boulders and shrubs and the angled paths of a Japanese garden do.

Such letters meant and mean much to both of us.

CHAPTER FIVE

Adding a Wing

B Y 1945 the need for a guest house became pressing. Our children were older, and it was unfair to ask one of them to give up a room for an overnight or weekend guest. The number of our guests increased dramatically once we moved into a Wright-designed house. Further, our overseas assignments resulted in an increase in numbers of visitors from abroad.

By then we thought a room for a live-in maid was not necessary, and the children no longer needed such care—even if it were findable and affordable. In addition, we both had enrolled in evening courses in woodworking and wanted a large workshop of our own. We asked Mr. Wright to develop new plans.

Our experience with delays during the initial building period prepared us for what might happen now. Fortunately, our time was overcommitted, and so we let Mr. Wright and the apprentices fit our project into their own very busy schedules of work.

The Wrights visited us late in May of 1946. We were able to discuss several problems of design for the new wing. On August 21, Mr. Wright wrote: "I am ashamed to have made you wait so long for plans." Finally a wire from Taliesin on September 28 brought welcome news: "Plans in airmail today." Most of these blueprints dealt with minor changes in the main house.

More plans arrived by the middle of October. We wrote to Mr. Wright:

The drawings arrived. . . . We are pleased with the . . . shop unit. However . . . enclosed is a drawing of proposed alterations. The suggestions are all internal, and made because of certain . . . needs. . . . If you accept the suggested changes, we believe that we shall be prepared to go ahead as soon as the building trades loosen up and permit us the necessary materials. . . . The material shortage is so acute that we are sure we shall not be able to start on the addition until spring. . . . The rain will be coming soon and it will

Pouring footing for chimney in shop, 1950   *Footing for southwest wall of shop*   *Jean Hanna at chimney of shop*

be just as well to wait until that is over. So . . . everything being O.K., we shall hope to begin on the addition about the first of March [1947]. It shouldn't take long to complete. We called Mr. Roberts, the best carpenter we had on the job during our 1937 construction, to see if he could supervise . . . but he has had a couple of heart attacks and is not well. However, he may be able to come down and see that the men do the job correctly.

This letter must have relieved any feeling of urgency at Taliesin, and we ourselves caused further delay. Besides teaching, publishing contracts demanded all our time and attention for the next year. Then, overseas assignments to the Panama Canal Zone, Germany, and the Philippines forced aside any effort to build the wing during 1947 and 1948. We told Mr. Wright our situation, and he laid the drawings aside.

At last we wrote to Mr. Wright on July 20, 1949:

Greetings! It certainly is wonderful to be back in our country, though we had a marvelous experience. . . .

There is much activity on our hill, now. Our friends, the Dodds, have started to build and at the same time we are having our hill dragged down . . . for our future guest room and shop. The bulldozer has about completed the leveling. We shall let the ground settle until next spring, when we hope to start building this addition. . . .

We aim to build the second layout you sent us, with a few slight revisions. For example, you will note by the enclosed sketch that we wish to enlarge the storage room next to the carport. Then we would like to leave a covered passage way between our place and Dodds. We had to simplify the guest room as you will note by the enclosed drawings.

We find the shop fireplace as drawn too elaborate either for our purse or our use. We need as simple a fireplace as is possible to construct. If this is

96

Outside stairway to shop　　　　　　*Shop roof*　　　　　　*Inside shop*

impossible, then we shall omit the fireplace all together.

Would you make the walls solid core board and batten like the Basset house or like ours with studs?

We finally reached agreement—Mr. Wright had drawn plans that incorporated our main requests, and we had been persuaded that fundamental unity with the main house must be preserved in the new wing.

Our earlier experience in trying to find a contractor did not encourage us to approach various builders. We thought perhaps we could be our own contractor again. We appealed to Mr. Wright for an apprentice to supervise the construction, but all were busy. Paul knew Stanford's director of planning, and discussed our problem with him. After studying the plans, Eldridge Spencer agreed to assist us through his architectural firm, Spencer and Ambrose. On January 23, 1950 they presented their terms, which we accepted:

. . . we will undertake the supervision of the construction of an addition to your residence. . . . We will also prepare whatever drawings and specifications are necessary for the proper execution of Mr. Wright's designs by a contractor and in addition we will prepare necessary contract documents, issue certificates of payment, keep the accounts of the cost of construction, and handle the general administration of the work.

We will undertake the above services for a fee based on our own office costs with the provision that our total fee will not exceed 8 percent of the cost of construction.

A standard American Institute of Architects' contract, twenty pages of specifications, and four addenda were developed for the contractor and ourselves. This contract called for completion in 120 days at a cost of $21,000, fee included.

Jack Seward of Mr. Spencer's architectural firm remained on site during construction; he proved to be a capable supervisor and our loyal friend. Construction began in late April and progressed on schedule. We made a few changes agreed to by all parties and approved by Mr. Wright. The final cost of our additional building was $22,250.

The guest house, entered off the carport, was an extension of the main house without being attached to it. Over the years scores of guests were thus provided with comfortable bedroom/sitting room, kitchenette, and bathroom. (The kitchenette enabled some guests to prepare breakfast at their leisure, if they so desired.) Furthermore, the hobby shop proved to be our pride and joy, a center for much leisure activity. Countless hours were spent there making everything from furniture to chess boards, from wooden lamps to pottery bowls. Our sons built sports gear and an assortment of youthful trappings. Later, as heads of families, they used the shop to make or repair baby furniture and office equipment. A group of Stanford student volunteers constructed toys for school children in the Philippines and for local children's hospitals. The hobby shop was a splendid place for occasional seminars. With the heavy machinery moved, work benches cleared off, and temporary tables set up, it proved ideal for eight people doing summer research and writing.

The shop was equipped with a radial arm saw, table saw, band saw, lathe, drill press, jointer, grinder, and vacuum cleaner. Cupboards along the west wall contained small electric tools, hand tools, and an assortment of hardware. Overhead, we stored fine hardwoods obtained while on duty in Latin America, Africa, and the Orient: narra, teak, dao, Honduras mahogany, ironwood, kamagon, and rosewood. Much of this was used to build furniture for our home. The northeast wall of the shop was glass above a thirty-two-foot-long work bench. The south end of the shop contained a simple sunken fireplace, into which we swept and burned sawdust and other rubbish. The north end of the shop was partitioned to house laundry, paint room, and lavatory.

The storeroom, reached under the roof, was a blessing; it was equipped with large cupboards that housed everything from camping equipment to cases of wine. It was ideal for storing garden furniture as well as all those sundry items that we planned to dispose of someday. Our multipurpose addition served us well.

Paul Hanna working in the shop

Shop equipment in place, 1953

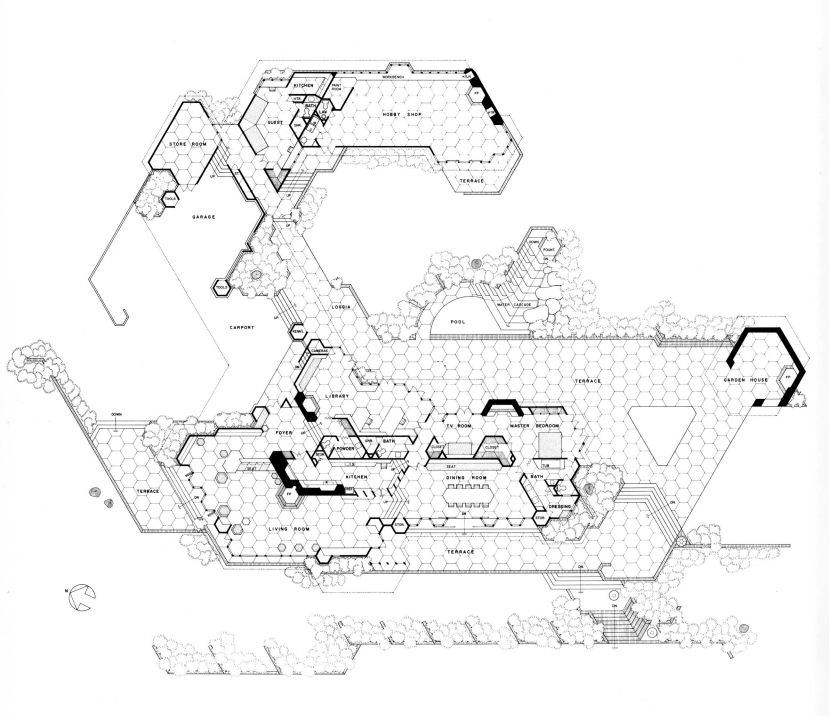

Plan of the Hanna House, 1957

100

The playroom terrace before hedge was removed

From foyer looking into living room

The living room

103

The living room

Living room fireplace

Dining room

106

The library

View of the west side

The garden terrace

CHAPTER SIX

Once the Children Leave

As foreseen when we started planning in 1935 and 1936, with each departing youngster we became increasingly eager to remake the house to suit the two of us. Finally in April, 1956, we wrote Mr. Wright that we were "seriously considering going ahead this spring and summer to complete the remodeling. . . . We hesitate to proceed without considerable guidance either through blueprints or through the presence of one of your apprentices. Would you please consider this matter and drop us a note?"

Mr. Wright answered: "Ask Aaron Green * to help you get started. I won't be out that way until next November 1."

On June 1, 1956, we wrote Mr. Wright:

Mr. Green came the other evening and we went over the proposed changes with him. He is going to study the original blueprints in order to determine just which walls can come down and how much work will be involved.

We are sure you will be pleased with the progress we have made recently in rejuvenating the house. We had the living room terrace jacked up, and put concrete foundations down eight feet. Somehow, Turner had neglected to allow for fill shrinkage. We had the brick flower box redone, and the ivy all torn off the brick walls. We have paved the little terrace off the living room and built a small fountain for the fish pond. We also rebuilt the storm-damaged wall around the big cypress tree that goes through the roof.

Inside we . . . refinished the walls in the foyer, living room, and dining room with a wax-based varnish, and cleaned the fireplace chimney.

We are getting busy on the alterations for the rest of the house.

We would like to jack up the terrace off the dining room. That will be a major operation, but if we are as successful as we were with the living room terrace, we'll be very happy. . . .

Oh, yes, we forgot to tell you that the Japanese stone lanterns are beautiful and a huge success. Unfortunately, some youngsters out on a lark tipped over the one at the driveway entrance and smashed it. We couldn't get another one just like it, but found one at Gump's Store which we think is even more beautiful. (Aaron doesn't like it and thinks you won't; we think you will.)†

* Mr. Wright's West Coast representative at that time.

† Mr. Wright did like it.

We have read and thoroughly enjoyed both *The Story of the Tower* and Olgivanna's *The Struggle Within*.

On August 24 we wrote:

Jean and I are leaving on the twenty-second of September for the Orient. We'll be going through Europe and returning home just before Christmas.

We have been talking with Aaron Green concerning the remodeling of Honeycomb. We plan now to start the reconstruction early in January, just as soon as we can make final arrangements after our return.

We are still hoping that you can send out one of the apprentices to be with us for about two months during reconstruction. If this is utterly impossible because of the press of work of higher priority, then we are hoping you can give us additional blueprints to guide the contractor. We are hoping that Mr. Green can give us a little supervision from time to time but are fully aware of the tremendous demands on his time and energy and believe that he would feel better if we had an apprentice here on the job.

At the same time we wrote to Aaron Green:

You will see from the enclosed carbon that we are still asking Mr. Wright to loan us an apprentice. If this doesn't work out, then we certainly want to follow through on the plan we discussed with you as an alternative, namely, that you assign us your head carpenter to manage the job and make an arrangement with us whereby we buy some of your supervisory time.

On January 9, 1957, we revived our communication with Mr. Wright:

We are back home after three months in Europe and Asia on government contract work for Stanford.

We are now eager to get started on remodeling the bedrooms and study section of our house. Can the following things happen?
—More detail drawings developing the ideas contained in the sketches given you recently.
—We need the guidance of one of your Fellows. Mr. Green reported that you

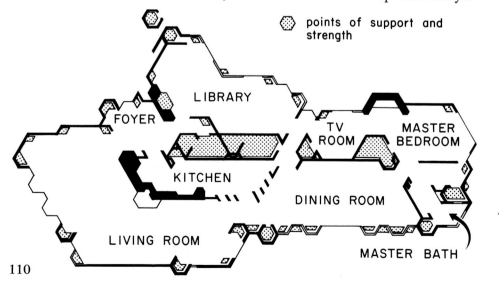

A simplified plan of the house

were considering sending David Dodge. This would be excellent. Could he start about February 11?

—I want to come to Taliesin West for Saturday afternoon through Sunday noon, January 26–27, to discuss final arrangements 1) for detail drawings mentioned above and 2) with David Dodge. Will you be at Taliesin at that time?

We had accumulated ideas on how to revamp the interior of the Hanna House to suit the changed condition of our family.

We listed the room changes proposed as follows:

ORIGINAL		PROPOSED
Study and master bedroom	to become	Library
Master bath	to become	Powder room
Boys' bath	to become	Utility bath
#1 son's bedroom	to become	Guest bedroom
#2 son's bedroom and daughter's bedroom	to become	Master bedroom
Daughter's bath and TV den	to become	Master bath

Dining room, living room, foyer, and kitchen to remain as in 1957.

Mr. Wright encouraged our ideas. Our suggested rearrangement can be seen in Figure A; Figure B shows how Mr. Wright was able to simplify and particularize our efforts.

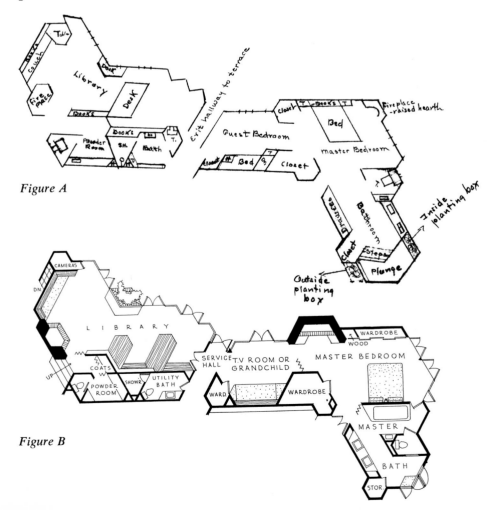

Figure A

Figure B

The changes suggested to Mr. Wright added up to what appeared to be a major job of reconstruction. However, with the exception of two new chimneys and fireplaces, and moving out the east wall half a hexagonal unit to enlarge the new master bedroom, there were no alterations in the basic floor plan or structure of the building.

Mr. Wright had designed the original mechanics of the structure well. Never was dismantling so easy. The screws were extracted from the horizontal battens and the vertical corner pieces. We removed the top batten, then a board, then the next lower batten, and so on until the bottom board and batten had been removed and all material carefully stored for reuse. The same careful procedure removed soffit, jambs, and studs. Doors were piano-hinged and easily detached. One might say that remodeling was primarily a job of extracting and replacing screws.

More difficult features of remodeling were, of course, plumbing, heating, and the electrical systems. We installed a more modern set of gas-fired heating units. The original three-zone system of controls and ducts remained intact. We replaced the old water-heater tank with a more efficient model. These alterations required detailed blueprints.

While waiting for drawings and specifications to arrive from Taliesin, we pondered the question: to contract or not to contract? We had experienced both procedures. We concluded we should not afford contractor's fees. Familiar as we were with the concept of Mr. Wright's design, we believed we could undertake the alteration with the aid of a top-grade carpenter, an apprentice-supervisor from Taliesin, and an occasional visit by Mr. Wright.

We did not have to search long to find a top-grade carpenter. Mr. Leonard Marinello had worked for Mr. Green for some years; however, Marinello could not start our job for two months. We were impatient to begin, and were able to procure, temporarily, the services of a carpenter we knew, and through him, a second man.

We had submitted drawings of the remodeling to the planning office of Stanford and asked permission to undertake the work. On January 25, 1957, Mr. Harry Sanders, associate director of planning, wrote to Mr. Dwight Adams, assistant business manager, the following letter:

At your request, this office has reviewed with Dr. Hanna plans for the proposed alterations to his residence at 737 Frenchman's Road.

The plans, prepared by Architect Frank Lloyd Wright, call for interior changes which, in effect, will create three rooms in 2,000 square foot area now occupied by six rooms on the southeast side of the house. A rearrangement of plumbing fixtures and the construction of two new fireplaces also are involved. All of the work proposed will take place under the existing roof and, with one exception, within existing exterior walls. The one exception calls for the relocation of one short wall 22 inches outside of its existing line.

The plans proposed for the Hanna Residence meet the approval of the Planning Office. In discussing them with Dr. Hanna, we pointed out the need for him or a representative to contact the proper authorities regarding a building permit.

On January 28 we received official approval from Stanford for remodeling, and a university loan of $20,000 to pay for the work.

However, acting on our own we did make mistakes. For instance, Paul neglected to obtain a building permit, even though the Stanford planning office had asked him to do so. We discovered our oversight later, and Paul persuaded the county authorities that no harm had been intended or done. They issued the permit.

We and the two carpenters began to tear out built-in furniture, to disconnect plumbing and electrical fixtures, and to remove interior redwood walls. At this point we discovered an infestation of termites. We wrote Mr. Wright on February 26:

We received the blueprints. Thank you. Just to prove that we are really serious about this business, the day the plans arrived, we had completed removing the toilets, basins, and the tubs from the two bathrooms. As of today, we have one new toilet and basin set, and tomorrow will have another toilet and basin installed.

We are rapidly packing up and putting things away so that we can start removing the interior walls. We found carpenters who will do many jobs that need to be done while we are waiting for Mr. Green's men to complete his house.

We were feeling a bit worried lest we had jumped into this too hastily, but a discovery Sunday convinced us that we must go ahead at once. Namely: termites! We found the studs of one wall of a bedroom badly perforated by termites, and fear that some studs of the study walls may be likewise. The workmen in 1937 had not creosoted every stud. Termites don't care much for the redwood, but like the fir studs. So it is a good thing that we are taking down walls. This time we must treat *every* stud with chemicals.

We were able to employ master bricklayers from the state of Washington to build the two new chimneys.

About the second week of work, Paul was invited to consult with the Hawaiian State Board of Education. No sooner had he left than Jean, impatient with the lack of progress, ordered five carpenters from the local union hiring hall to augment the crew of two.

Again the men had to be educated to use the 120-degree angle iron in place of the "tried and true" square. It was rough going. Jean worked along with the carpenters, encouraging and occasionally reprimanding. We sometimes paid to have a wall put up wrong, paid to have it taken down, and paid to have it put up right. But at the end of a week the carpenters had the hang of the module and were working well.

One morning two men appeared at the house; they introduced themselves as officials of the Carpenters' Union. Jean greeted them and introduced them to the work crew. There was a sudden change in atmosphere; one of the visitors said, "Mrs. Hanna, I'm afraid you are in serious trouble." Unwittingly, Jean had violated union rules: union carpenters and non-union bricklayers were working side-by-side. Jean stubbornly insisted she had a right to hire anyone she pleased in her own home. The carpenters hadn't worked for weeks; they were happy to be earning a living. No use. Jean was given an ultimatum: get rid of the bricklayers or the union would pull all the carpenters off the job. Jean told them she'd think about it. The officials returned, every day for three days, each time threatening. At the end of the week Jean gave the Carpenters' Union her answer: the bricklayers would remain. As the carpenters regretfully gathered up their tools, Jean thanked them for their work. Not a man rebuked her for choosing to keep the bricklayers. Paul arrived home to find a distraught wife. He was pleased with the progress, sorry for the harassment, thankful the bricklayers had been kept, and would talk with the union.

We had been pressing Mr. Wright to send us an apprentice; we might be doing some things wrong. At last Gene Masselink wired us: "David Dodge will arrive Monday evening [March 11] or Tuesday morning. He is driving." We were pleased Mr. Wright was sending David; we had known him for several years. He was to stay until the job was finished. Unfortunately he had to leave early, and we were on our own again during the last months of construction.

During his stay, David's sensitive discrimination sometimes posed a problem. For instance, Paul insisted that the new firepits be made of firebrick rather than common red brick. David did not like either the pale color or the large size of firebricks. We won this argument with the assistance of the master bricklayer. David then went to town, bought paint, and covered the firebrick with a proper sooty black.

David was frugal. Rather than purchase a new door to go between the new master bedroom and the small guestroom, he proposed to use doors left over from the remodeling. He devised a handsome, heavy folding door and supervised the carpenters assembling it. When the door was completed, Paul sent David to purchase an overhead track to carry this door. When he returned, Paul asked if the track he purchased was the best he could find. David replied, "No, there was a heavier track but I considered it overpriced." Two months after David left we had to replace the light track with the heavier one. We appreciated David's attempt to save us money, but on occasion parsimony proved expensive. David has long since become a successful practicing architect, we might add.

Leonard Marinello, Mr. Green's man, was free by April 4 and came to work, accompanied by one carpenter. After a week we added several more carpenters. Mr. Marinello was an excellent cabinetmaker. He and the crew, like the crew of 1937, built well. Upon completing our job, he became a successful licensed contractor but was never too busy to return to us for some special task.

We had never liked the Nu-wood ceiling, an economy compromise in the 1937 construction. Mr. Wright's plans had called for redwood ceilings, but we had feared that redwood would seem dark and heavy; we liked to look up to a light surface. Years later, in 1952, we had found a material in Manila that appealed: a cloth, called saguran, woven of native fiber. We ordered several bolts, and when they arrived, the cloth was pasted to the Nu-wood in the living room and dining room. Mr. Wright approved the results. Then, when we were remodeling in 1957, we sent for six more bolts of saguran and had ceilings throughout the main house covered with this material.

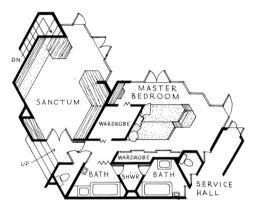

For years we had coped with circumscribed space in the study. Only the thought that it was temporary comforted us. Even the closet occupied space that should have been a fireplace. Now Mr. Wright's floor plan for the new enlarged library delighted us. The removal of a nonbearing wall between the study and our bedroom provided a spacious new room, appropriately now called library. All available wall space was lined with bookshelves and cabinets, while the east side of the room was plate glass. As throughout the house, hot and cold air vents were incorporated in the two new chimney stacks. A built-in couch was remodeled and cushions made for back and seat, covered in fabric from India. This couch could be used as an extra bed.

Original master bedroom plan, top. After children left, partitions were removed to form large library area, below.

Mr. Wright suggested fireplaces with regular floor-level hearths in the library and master bedroom. Jean flew to Taliesin West to ask Mr. Wright for raised hearths with hobs. In accordance with the myths about "no compromise" with Mr. Wright's ideas, she should not have gone.

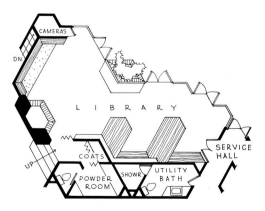

The working library

When Jean arrived Mr. Wright was napping, so she wandered into the drafting room to talk to the apprentices and mentioned raised hearths. She was told Mr. Wright would not design them, and she should forget it.

When Mr. Wright was available, he and Jean sat by the pool, and, after talking about a number of things, Jean came to the point: "Mr. Wright, we'd like to have a raised hearth in each fireplace." Mr. Wright asked, "Why do you want raised hearths?" Jean explained: a raised hearth in the library would permit us to view the fire from both of our desks, and the hob would provide extra seating and space for a statue; a raised hearth in the master bedroom would allow an eye-level view of the fire from both of our beds and also from the bed in the grandchild's room.

Mr. Wright listened carefully and said, "That sounds like a perfectly legitimate reason. You'll have your raised hearths."

Mr. Wright had designed two large desks with redwood tops for the new library. However, our experience demonstrated that this wood is too soft for desk tops; any weight dropped on redwood leaves a dent. As it happened, we had brought with us from the Philippines ten narra boards, each 10 feet long, 24 inches wide, and 1¼ inches thick. These boards of fine hardwood were planed, cut to conform to the hexagonal module, braced underneath with steel ribs, and set on top of two-drawer metal filing cabinets. These tops blended well with the other woods used in the library. Even with much labor by both Hannas this room involved considerable expense, but it was both practical and beautiful.

The library became a much-used room in which we visited with friends, held conferences, carried on research, viewed TV, read, wrote, had a snack, or just relaxed. A wood fire burned in the fireplace day and night for eight months of the year.

Relocating the master bedroom at the east end of the house proved a happy move. At the head of the big new bed we built a recessed shelf holding reading lamps, switches for the burglar alarm system and outside flood lights, telephone, and spare electrical outlets. Controls for heat and room lighting were within easy reach.

The bed actually consisted of two twin-size, electrically operated hospital beds; one large bedspread covered them by day. For reading or for periods of extended confinement, these independently adjustable beds were most satisfying.

The beds were placed so that the morning sun welcomed us. Through the glass walls we could watch birds, squirrels, and racoons feeding, enjoy the flowering fruit trees, or admire the garden sculpture. On stormy mornings,

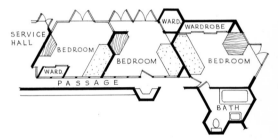

Plans showing three children's bedrooms in 1937, and conversion, in 1957, to master bedroom and television or grandchild's room.

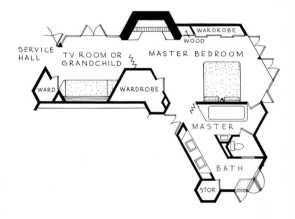

The master bedroom

racing clouds, rain, and swaying branches prompted us to build a glowing fire on the hearth. On stormy nights, with Aeroshades lowered, the cavelike atmosphere and flickering fire gave us a feeling of security and wellbeing.

The bedroom fireplace had an additional function. For a grandchild guest in the adjoining bedroom, the friendly fire at night banished any feeling of fear and strangeness.

We never ceased to find pleasure in witnessing changes from day to night, changes in the weather, changes in the seasons, and changes in the

118

moon cycles. Our childhood love of nature was fulfilled with Mr. Wright's design of our home.

Our new bathroom was large, comfortable, and fully equipped. When the two-lavatory counter was being readied, we suddenly remembered some ceramic tiles Paul had bought in Spain. The full set (a bullfight scene) just fitted between the wash basins, and the background color exactly matched that of the tiles being set on the counter.

The room formerly called the playroom now became the dining room. Appropriate furniture was designed and made. Carpeting was laid. Aero-shades, sliding on a horizontal track, were installed to cut out summer sun in the afternoon.

In this old play space, new activities took place. Family gatherings were enhanced by an extension table that could seat all sixteen family members,* or when fully extended, up to thirty-six guests. We entertained at university functions, using the dining room for stand-up cocktails or more formal luncheons and dinners.

The youngsters' book shelves had long since been converted to displaying chess sets, a Hanna hobby. Jean became tired of dusting more than fifty chess sets, so Paul made glass sliding doors to enclose the chessmen.

The only alteration to the kitchen consisted of removing one entry closet (between foyer and kitchen) and replacing it with a double-door entry to the kitchen from the foyer.

In the autumn of 1958 we invited Mr. Wright to visit us and pass on what had been accomplished. It was to be the last visit before his death. We proudly witnessed his satisfaction with the way "it all came together."

With the completion of our remodeled home we became more fully aware of the significance of what Mr. Wright had written in 1910:

The creative artist can but give color of his own likes and dislikes, his own soul to the thing he shapes. He gives his individuality, but will not prevent the building from being characteristic of those it was built to serve, because it necessarily is a solution of conditions they make, and it is made to serve their ends in their own way. Insofar as these conditions are peculiar in themselves, or sympathy exists between the clients and the architect, the building will be their building. It will be theirs much more truly than though in ignorant selfhood they had stupidly sought to use means they had not conquered to an end imperfectly foreseen. The architect, then, is their means, their technique and interpreter; the building an interpretation, if he is a true architect . . . .

The master bathroom

* With married sons and daughter, grandchildren, and the two of us.

119

Aerial view of the Hanna House, 1962

CHAPTER SEVEN

The Future of Our House

WE cannot be certain just when we realized that Mr. Wright had designed a masterpiece for us that deserved to be preserved for posterity. The National Trust for Historic Preservation had influenced our thinking, and we had read volumes on our American heritage. We knew that many important buildings had been seriously altered or destroyed because no plans had been made for their preservation and use after the original owners had departed. We were often asked about the ultimate disposition of our home. Such questions did not disturb us; the structure would outlive us by generations, provided we planned well for it.

Ray Lyman Wilbur, Stanford's president from 1916 to 1943, teased us by threatening to turn the house into a faculty club. We took this seriously enough to think about the day when we would no longer need our house. What then? Informally we talked with President Wilbur about our idea to give our home to the university as a memorial to Mr. Wright. He and other colleagues encouraged us. The Hanna House might become an important instructional and research component of the university program in art and architecture. Other possibilities came to mind as well:

—a conference center like the Johnson Wingspread House in Wisconsin;
—the residence of a university officer: the Robie House near the University of Chicago was proposed for the chancellor of that university;
—a museum for the work by and about Frank Lloyd Wright.

But we did not actively pursue the preservation concept for two decades. In 1959 we realized that the years were passing, and no long-range plans had been formulated for the Hanna House. We conferred with the university's general secretary, David Jacobson, and orally offered to give our home to the university. We suggested we might retain life interest, the house to be used, after we no longer needed it, as a center for teaching and research in architecture and art.

We had in mind another motive in giving the house to Stanford then,

Taliesin Fellowship visits the Hanna House

rather than after our deaths. We felt as did Edgar Kaufmann, jr., who transferred his famous Fallingwater House to the Western Pennsylvania Conservancy because "I can arrange for its proper preservation better now than after I'm gone."

In February, 1959, we received this letter from Mr. Jacobson:

After we talked in my office about the generous plans which you and Mrs. Hanna had in connection with the ultimate use of your house, I submitted the proposal, in confidence, to the appropriate authorities, including the Advisory Committee on Land and Building Development. I have just now received an answer, which is to the effect that it was agreed that it would be unwise to have buildings used for educational purposes and those used for private residences mixed in together, as it is believed that all structures in the faculty residential area should be one-family residences.

Needless to say, it would be more pleasant for me had the answer been in the affirmative. Even though it was not, I want to assure you both that we are most appreciative of your generous offer.

We concluded that this made good sense, and we came to the realization that the hard usage of buildings for instructional purposes would place a heavy load on our home, which could result in rapid deterioration. Thereafter, we expected the university might propose alternative uses acceptable to all concerned, but Mr. Jacobson's letter ended this phase of planning for the preservation of our home.

Soon after, we had several inquiries and offers from faculty and staff members to purchase our home. One newly appointed teacher spoke of having lived in a Wright-designed house in the East and his wish to dwell in such a house on the Stanford campus. He asked on what terms we might sell. While we welcomed the evidence that a Wright-designed residence had value in the Stanford marketplace, the house was not for sale; someday, somehow, we would find a way to preserve the house as a memorial to Mr. Wright. Our children were unselfishly in accord with giving our home to Stanford or a similar entity.

When we were working with *House Beautiful* in the preparation of the January 1963 issue, Elizabeth Gordon, the editor, urged us to make some statement for the magazine. Here is what was printed:

Hopefully—A Memorial to Frank Lloyd Wright

The Hannas are often asked about their intention concerning the ultimate disposition of their house. They realize that the structure will outlast them, and that its future should be planned for carefully.

They have entertained the idea of its permanent use as a teaching facility and research center for the arts. Possibly the germ for this idea lay in the frequent requests to open their home to student groups from the Art and Architecture departments of Stanford University, the University of California, British Columbia, and groups from many other institutions. Other possibilities for eventual use of the house came to mind as they contemplated the advantages of a Wright-designed house dedicated to education in the arts and architecture.

The Hannas have even speculated that some of the priceless collection of sixty years of Mr. Wright's architectural sketching and writing might finally find a permanent home in such a Wright memorial.

Regardless of anyone's personal feeling about Mr. Wright and his work, the fact remains that he exerted a powerful influence upon the art and architecture of the world, and somehow a selected few of his residential buildings ought to be preserved for posterity, as examples of that influence.

In November, 1964, we received a letter from the American Institute of Architects:

In 1960, a special Frank Lloyd Wright Memorial Committee was appointed by the President of the American Institute of Architects to select certain American projects designed by Mr. Wright and recommended these buildings to be restored or preserved as a part of our American architectural culture.

This special committee worked directly with Mrs. Frank Lloyd Wright and the Taliesin associated architects which resulted in 17 projects being selected and approved by the A.I.A. at the 1960 national convention.

Subsequently, through the cooperation of the Taliesin group, negative photostatic copies of the working drawings of these projects were forwarded to the A.I.A. in Washington where they will permanently remain in the vaults of the A.I.A. archives. One positive set of prints of each project is expected to be available at the Octagon House for study and exhibition on the premises in Washington, D.C.*

As a present owner of one of these important projects, it is the intention of the A.I.A. to offer you tangible evidence in the way of a small plaque or certificate which should be installed in a permanent manner in an appropriate location on the building.

The plaque was brought to Palo Alto while we were on sabbatical leave. As it turned out, our absence proved fortunate. Stanford was at the moment planning a summer arts festival, and the university festival staff worked with us and the A.I.A. in selecting speakers and preparing guest lists for the ceremonial presentation of the plaque. Our private hope was that the occasion might persuade Stanford University to accept our home as a gift and thus assure its preservation as an outstanding example of the work of Frank Lloyd Wright.

The *Stanford Daily* carried a typical release on Thursday, May 26, 1966:

Architects Pick Local House for Frank Wright Memorial

A Frank Lloyd Wright-designed house on the Stanford University campus will be designated an architectural monument by the American Institute of Architects and opened to public tours on July 9 as part of the Stanford Summer Festival of the Arts.

Wright is one of the creative geniuses being honored in the eight-week festival, June 22–Aug. 13, on the theme: "20th Century Innovations."

The Paul R. Hanna home at 737 Frenchman's Road was designed by Wright in 1936. It has a hexagonal theme which Wright felt gave fluid continuity to staged development of the home's four separate buildings. The entire living-entertaining center has few, if any, right angles in it.

The AIA is honoring Wright this year by placing plaques at 17 of his most celebrated buildings, including the Hanna home.

The Stanford dedication ceremony will be attended by guests of the AIA and University only. However, starting at 4:30 p.m. July 19, the Hannas will open the house for viewing by the public for three hours. Tickets for the tour are free but limited, and must be obtained in writing from the Summer Festivals Office, Stanford University.

Hanna holds the Lee L. Jacks Professorship in Child Education at Stanford.

Wright's works will be reviewed along with others of the 20th century in classes offered by the University's Art and Architecture Department during the summer quarter.

Display of plaques from the A.I.A., Stanford University, and Historic House Association of America

---

* *A set of drawings of the Hanna House has yet to be placed in the A.I.A. archives.*

124

Other 20th century innovators in music, drama, literature, motion pictures and art will be given detailed study and interpretation in seminars, classes, workshops and professional performances during the festival. Information on these programs also is available from the Festivals Office.

The account of the award ceremony is to be found in the microfilm. Happily the festival did create a favorable attitude toward the preservation of our dwelling.

During the autumn of 1966, we conferred with our attorney, our son John Paul Hanna, about the legal problems of a charitable donation of the house to Stanford. The discussions were broadened to include officers of the Crocker National Bank and the legal division of Stanford, as well as President Sterling and the general secretary of the university. Certain academic colleagues were of great assistance in exploring possible uses of the buildings. Furthermore, we sought advice from the National Trust for Historic Preservation in Washington, D.C. Giving the house to the National Trust seemed complicated, since the dwelling stood on leased Stanford land. The Trust advised on provisions to include in a formal donation to Stanford.

We came to the firm conclusion that we preferred the home to be the residence of a distinguished visiting university professor. Annually, Stanford could invite a man or woman of world distinction to be its guest in residence. Such scholar, leader, or creative genius would live on campus, sharing ideas and inspiration with faculty and students, offering seminars or lectures as desired and appropriate.

Then in December of 1966 we donated a 20-percent interest in our house to Stanford University. In 1969 we gave an additional 25 percent and in 1971 another 25 percent, leaving a final 30-percent interest to complete this transaction.

In preparing to make the final gift, we were surprised but not discouraged when the general secretary advised us that our formal deed could state our desire that the Hanna House might serve a distinguished visiting professor, but that the trustees must have final power to decide how our gift would be used: "A donor may not legally commit a recipient." Thus the deed should indicate a range of possible uses, including our plan of a residence for a visiting guest professor, but must clearly state that acceptance of our gift would not legally bind the trustees to follow our intentions.

We were assured orally by friends in the university administration that they agreed with and would carry out our plans to have the Hanna House used as the residence of a distinguished visiting scholar. With these oral assurances, we proceeded to prepare the final deed of gift and related documents; these form part of the microfilmed archive.

Early in 1972 we began to consider the policies and agencies that would govern, maintain, and staff the Hanna House and that would select and serve the distinguished guest. In other words, who would administer the endowments, and according to what principles? For a year and a half we sought guidance from the university administration and from trusted friends.

To guarantee that the Hanna House would be carefully maintained, in a letter of June 8, 1973, President Lyman created a Board of Governors, who would be concerned with overseeing "the use, management, maintenance, repair, and protection of Hanna-Honeycomb House, its furnishings, and its grounds. . . . The Board shall also make recommendations to the President regarding the expenditures of funds . . . for the care of Honeycomb House . . . and may suggest names for appointment of an endowed visiting professor" to live in the house.

The board's overseeing would provide continuity of persons with knowledge of and sympathy for authentic preservation of an architectural landmark. Many important historic properties have been altered by well-intentioned but uninformed individuals, to the great detriment of the original character of the work. This house by Frank Lloyd Wright deserves to be preserved without change, as an example of his creative work.

Evidence that Stanford considers the Board of Governors to be a significant factor in carrying out the program of "Distinguished Visiting Professorship and Residence" is found·in the president's appointments to the board. He named the provost as chairman of the governing board, along with the dean of humanities and science, the dean of one of the other six professional schools, the vice president for business and finance, the vice president for development, two or more members of the faculty, and the Hannas, who would attend and participate (without vote) in all meetings of the board.

A "Campaign for Stanford" to raise $300 million in endowment was then underway. The development office of Stanford prepared documents to use in soliciting $500,000 in endowment funds for the permanent upkeep of the house and a separate endowment for the distinguished visiting university professor who would occupy the house. Regrettably, no funds were raised for this program during the campaign. The Board of Governors was not convened during 1974, the chairman deciding that no action on

the property or the professorship was possible until the two endowments were available.

On February 21, 1974, we sent a letter of intent to the university trustees, from which we quote:

It is our desire to have this architectural piece stand permanently on the Stanford University campus as a living example of the philosophy and of the design principle of this genius. We have faith in the present and future persons responsible for the welfare of this University and are confident that they understand the intent of the donors in wishing to have this architectural treasure preserved as a feature of Stanford. Because of this faith in both the place history will assign the architect, and in the wisdom of those who will make decisions regarding the preservation and the use of this building, we are not specifying the mechanism by which our wishes shall be carried out. . . .

In any decision regarding its optimum use, we again stress that we wish the original buildings to be preserved as an example of Wright's architectural philosophy and execution. We would be disappointed were the buildings to be altered in such ways as to destroy the original unity and organic relation to the land and climate. We would hope that any alterations necessary would be executed under the architectural direction of persons familiar and in sympathy with Mr. Wright's principles as shown in the sketches and drawings made by Mr. Wright for the house.

In making this gift to Stanford, we wish to be understood as desiring the residence to be preserved in such a manner that it will serve educational ends. We would view its sale to a private party as defeating this purpose.

It is our hope that the University administration will seek funds to endow the costs of maintaining and preserving the buildings and grounds in first class condition. Because of the special nature of the building and grounds, these costs might be higher than for an ordinary residence, and this fact should be considered in permanent funding and in annual budgeting.

We assume the University will insure the property in such manner that it could be restored to its original condition were it damaged by fire, wind, earthquake, or other causes.

We desire that the buildings and grounds permanently display the art objects that the donors leave thereon and therein. To the extent possible and consistent with the use to which the University might from time to time make of the property, we wish the whole always to create an environment of calm, of dignity, of repose, of beauty, and of harmony. We are confident that those responsible for the administration of the property will be equally dedicated to the preservation of one of the best works of Frank Lloyd Wright.

All of the foregoing is intended only as an expression of our hopes and is not intended as binding on the University.

We make this gift unconditionally.

Upon receipt of the above letter and deeds, President Lyman wrote us a letter of acknowledgment. We responded to the president with this letter:

Thank you for your gracious letter of January 19 concerning the remainder gift of our campus home.

As soon as we can move into the proposed faculty/staff apartments, we will give up our life interest in our home and then it can be used as a part of the package for the visiting professor who will be a distinguished world figure. In the meantime, we are delighted to be able to assist in the reconstruction of the hobby shop and guest quarters as a permanent apartment for a caretaker couple who will care for the premises and serve the distinguished visiting professor. . . .

As time went on the documents in our files refer more often to a distinguished visiting professor, but the first concept was broader. We believed that a distinguished guest, if truly of world stature, would be acceptable even if not an accredited professor. Nevertheless it was clearly easier to satisfy the university administration, and easier to approach potential donors, with the academic title as an index of quality.

After signing and recording these documents, it was essential to seek an endowment for the staffing, maintenance, and preservation of the house and another endowment for the fees and expenses of the distinguished guest. We offered to carry out certain tasks that we believed would contribute to the objectives set forth in the letter of transmittal.

We would attempt to raise $500,000 for a permanent endowment for the house, the income from which would assure that the property would be kept in near mint condition and employ a caretaker couple to manage the property, serve the distinguished guests living in the house, and help interpret the house to the public who wished to visit it.

We would assist Stanford in raising $1 million as a permanent endowment for the chair, the income from which would pay the salary and expenses of the distinguished visiting university professor.

We would continue to live in the house, paying rent for two years while we supervised the reconstruction of the shop into an apartment for the caretaker couple. The plans for the remodeling would be drawn by the Frank Lloyd Wright Associated Architects.

We then flew to Japan to raise funding. We have many friends in Japan who are enthusiastic about the architecture of Frank Lloyd Wright; several of them had visited our house and expressed interest in its preservation. One was the Japanese architect Raku Endo, former apprentice of Mr. Wright at Taliesin, the son of Arato Endo, Mr. Wright's chief assistant in building the Imperial Hotel* and other structures in Japan. Raku Endo and Mitsuya Goto had been classmates at Jiyu Gakuen Secondary School in Tokyo, and Frank Lloyd Wright had designed the elegant building of this famous school. Goto understandably had developed a great interest in Mr. Wright and his work. Mr. Goto was now a prominent international officer of the Nissan Motor Company. In Tokyo he graciously introduced us to his associates in the firm. Thereafter, Mr. Yutaka Katayama, chairman of the board of Nissan Motor Corporation in the United States, accompanied by Mr. Reid Briggs, legal counsel for Nissan Motor Company and a Stanford alumnus, gave us pleasure by visiting our home. Mr. Katayama was enthusiastic about the house and our hopes for its future. Following him came our friend Mr. Goto, who also responded encouragingly to our plans.

In October, 1975, we moved from our Wright-designed home into a condominium a few blocks closer to the heart of the campus. No funding was available at that time for the long-term project at the Hanna House.

On October 2, 1975, we heard that a decision had been made by the president of Stanford that the Hanna House would shelter the provost of the university and his family. The president wrote to members of the Board of Governors:

I have felt for some time that the University needed a second official residence occupied by the Provost. The requirements for receiving University guests and the demands to host University receptions, many of them involving fund-raising, are greater than can be accommodated by the President and the Lou Henry Hoover House alone. The Provost is a University officer who, in order adequately to fulfill his responsibilities, really must be here on campus. I

* *We joined our friends in trying, unsuccessfully, to save the Imperial from demolition.*

have decided, therefore, to designate the Honeycomb House as the Provost's residence and, at my request, Bill and Pat Miller are in the process of moving in.

This designation for Hanna-Honeycomb House will continue until we are successful in acquiring the necessary funds to initiate the Visiting Professor program. When the happy event becomes imminent, we shall begin a search for a new residence for the Provost.

Most of you attended a dinner for Mr. Goto last spring. We retain strong hopes that a major gift for Honeycomb House will be forthcoming and that it will represent a significant step toward our final goal. We will keep you posted on our efforts.

When first we heard of the decision to move the provost into our house we agreed that, as an interim solution, it was good, and we said so publicly. However, we were disappointed that during the occupancy of the then provost, the Board of Governors was convened only once in the three years. Changes in the house were made without consultation, the result of logical but, we felt, shortsighted decisions. A new roof was installed in 1977, side-stepping the hope of re-creating the original copper roof laid in 1937. New carpets were laid wall-to-wall, contrary to Mr. Wright's architectural concept that floor coverings should not hide the hexagonal floor units around the perimeter of the living room. It was such uninformed drifting away from the original character of the house that we had tried to avoid with the establishment of a Board of Governors.

Our friends in Japan worked on. Mr. Goto's and Mr. Katayama's encouragement was such that the general secretary of Stanford prepared an expanded brochure in Japanese and in English, which was presented by President Lyman to President Hiroshi Majima of the Nissan Motor Corporation in the United States and to Board Chairman Katsuji Kawamata of Nissan Motor Company, Ltd., in Tokyo. President Lyman's letter of August 20, 1976, to Chairman Kawamata follows:

I am writing now to submit to you and the Nissan Motor Co., Ltd., a proposal that I had hoped to be able to present personally.

The proposal involves the establishment at Stanford University of a Distinguished Visiting Professorship and, as a perquisite of that Professorship, the privilege of residing in Hanna-Honeycomb House, an architectural masterpiece designed by Frank Lloyd Wright and famed throughout the world as the first and best of his creations to employ the hexagonal scheme of design.

Hanna-Honeycomb House lies at the heart of our proposal. Commissioned originally in 1935 by Professor and Mrs. Paul Hanna, and later deeded by them as a gift to the University in 1974, the residence is located on the Stanford campus. The University is proud of the House which attracts visitors from all over the globe. We feel that the pleasure and distinction of living in Hanna-Honeycomb House during a period of residence at Stanford would add greatly to the attractiveness of the Visiting Professorship and would insure our continued ability to attract men or women of all nationalities who possess that high degree of international eminence that we are seeking. This is the background against which I would like to request of the Nissan Motor Co., Ltd., an endowment grant in the amount of $500,000 to maintain, preserve, and improve the structures and grounds of Hanna-Honeycomb House.

As the other major element of this proposal, Stanford hopes to establish a new form of endowed position: a Distinguished Visiting University Professorship. This would serve the University as a whole rather than any single School or Department. We conceive of it as a post of the very highest honor and prestige which would be held for all or most of an academic year by scholars, artists, or public figures of worldwide repute from many fields of professional endeavor and from many countries. I would like to request of the Nissan Motor Co., Ltd., an endowment in support of this Distinguished Visiting University Professorship in the amount of $1,000,000.

I am submitting this proposal in the light of Stanford's earlier discussions with Nissan that you doubtless recall and of the more detailed documentation prepared at that time. I enclose a copy of this for ready reference. It would be our hope, of course, that the name of Nissan could be conspicuously associated with both the Residence and the Professorship.

Since this proposal involves a large sum of money, I might mention that often gifts of this size are made in installments over a period of years. If, however, a firm pledge for the full endowment over an agreed time were received, it might be possible to activate the program in the fairly near future.

May I add a few words about Stanford. We are, as you may know, among the two or three leading private universities in the United States. For example, our Graduate School of Business—under the direction of Dean Arjay Miller, formerly President of the Ford Motor Company—and our School of Education are ranked first in the country by authoritative national surveys, our School of Engineering is second, our School of Medicine third, and so on. Stanford is, therefore, without a doubt the most distinguished private university in the entire western half of the United States. Our location on the eastern shores of the Pacific Ocean naturally orients us toward the West and toward Japan. Our ties with Japan go back to 1900 and have multiplied in the succeeding years. . . .

On December 13, 1976, President Lyman received the official announcement from Chairman Katsuji Kawamata of the Nissan Motor Company, Ltd., that Stanford would receive an endowment.

You have followed up on our conversation with a formal request for financial assistance from Nissan which was contained in your letter of August 20, 1976. I am pleased to inform you that we will make available $500,000 to your university through Nissan Motor Corporation in U.S.A. I hope it will be used as an endowment grant to maintain, preserve, and improve the structures and grounds of Hanna-Honeycomb House so that the distinguished visiting professor can be housed there. I regret that we are not in a position to provide an endowment in support of the distinguished visiting professorship, which you had also requested.

There followed a series of exchanges among the Hannas, officials of Stanford University, and the management of Nissan Motor Company, Ltd. These letters resulted in the formal presentation by Mr. Majima at the Hanna House on March 1, 1977, of an endowment check for $500,000. A commemorative plaque recording the gift was placed, permanently, in the foyer of the house.

Mr. Katayama, speaking at the presentation luncheon, expressed his enthusiasm for the project and looked forward to the time when the first visiting scholar would occupy the chair and reside in Hanna House. The best of sentiments were expressed by both donor and recipients. Frank Lloyd Wright's influence permeated the festive luncheon and American-Japanese appreciation of Frank Lloyd Wright's architecture was reaffirmed.

Soon thereafter, our friends in Tokyo informed us that negotiations were under way to have several motor companies in Japan join in endowing the chair for the distinguished visiting university professor to live in the house. In the midst of these discussions, another request for endowment was made to these same motor companies by another Stanford program, for endowments for a chair in Japanese studies. Our friends in Tokyo were confused by the competing appeals. As a result, our project languished once again.

In December, 1978, we heard from President Lyman:

I write to report the actions I am taking on the Hanna-Honeycomb House following Bill and Pat Miller's return to their own residence in mid-January. While we continue to seek donors for the distinguished professorship, it is certain that we will not be successful before January, and I do not wish to have the house remain vacant for any substantial period of time.

Quite fortuitously, we have found a way of insuring the proper supervision of the house and simultaneously addressing other needs. I suspect you have heard that we have appointed a new Director of Athletics—Andy Geiger—who takes office on the second of January. It occurred to some of us that the Geigers might be willing to assume responsibility for the Hanna-Honeycomb House for the six- to nine-month period, when they would otherwise be renting a home. We approached them with the idea, and they agreed to it; I must say that I am delighted . . . a senior University officer will continue to oversee, and be accountable for, the Hanna-Honeycomb House. The University will provide a housekeeper to insure that the proper level of house maintenance is sustained.

I hope you are not only pleased with this action, but remain assured that the University intends to oversee your extraordinary gift with all possible care and attention.

We were pleased to know that again a wise interim decision had been made by the president. The Geigers consulted the Hannas about the house, and we regained hope for the long-range project.

On April 18, 1979, the university newspaper informed its readers that:

[Donald] Kennedy will return to the University this summer following his June resignation [as commissioner of the U.S. Food and Drug Administration]. He and his wife, Jeanne, plan to live in Hanna House, a Frank Lloyd Wright creation on campus, where the provost has traditionally lived.

We exchanged friendly letters with the Kennedys, and they moved into Hanna House in August, 1979. They proved to be sympathetic and appreciative occupants.

In 1980, upon the resignation of President Richard Lyman, the Board of Trustees of Stanford University appointed Provost Donald Kennedy to succeed him in office. The Kennedys would eventually move to the Lou Henry Hoover House, the official residence of the university president. Thus, undoubtedly, the Hanna House would again be occupied by an interim tenant.

Unfortunately, no firm schedule has been formulated for the remodeling of the Hanna House shop as a residence for a caretaker couple. Under contract, drawings for this remodeling have been prepared by the Taliesin Associated Architects and deposited in the University Planning Office. The Nissan endowment was given for the apartment, for a caretaker's salary, and for the maintenance and improvement of Hanna House.

The Board of Governors appointed in 1973 to advise on the use of the Hannas' gift of their house, has been inactive since 1974. This important supervisory body should be convened to oversee the preservation of the property and to guide the policy regarding the distinguished visitor. The Board of Governors should direct the remodeling of the hobby shop into an apartment for a caretaker.

When Stanford obtains the funds (increased to $1.5 million) for the endowed visiting professor, the Board will be responsible for 1) recommending to the President appropriate candidates for the chair, and 2) monitoring the conditions supporting the distinguished guest.

We, the Hannas, remain hopeful that our dream may be fulfilled in our lifetime. Such long-range cooperative endeavors are the essence of great communities, justifying the pains, adjustments, and privileges that have been features of our life with the Hanna House on the campus of Stanford University.

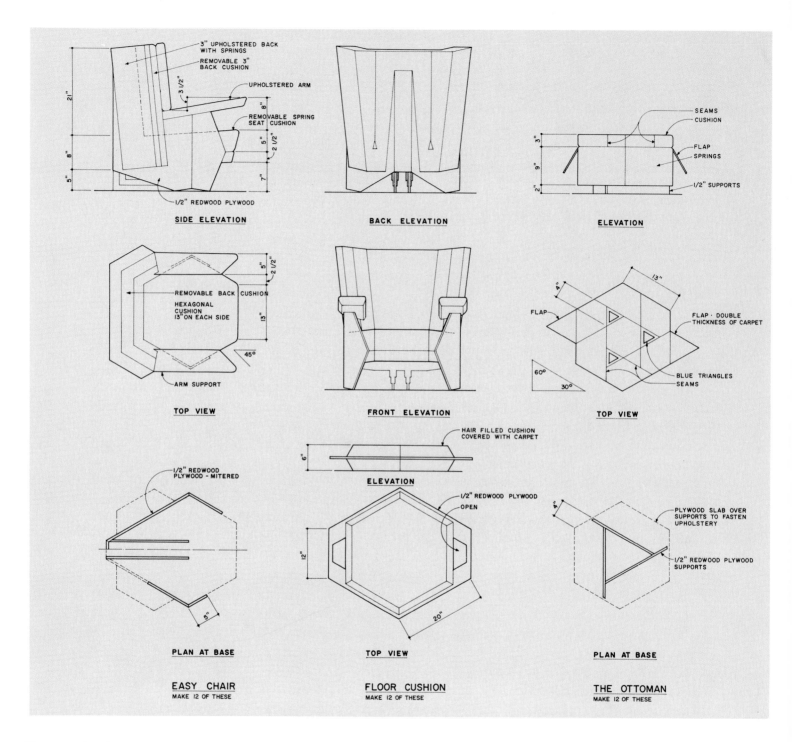

3" UPHOLSTERED BACK
WITH SPRINGS

REMOVABLE 3"
BACK CUSHION

UPHOLSTERED ARM

3 1/2"

21"

REMOVABLE SPRING
SEAT CUSHION

8"

5"

8"

5 1/2"

2 1/2"

7"

5"

1/2" REDWOOD PLYWOOD

SIDE ELEVATION

BACK ELEVATION

SEAMS

CUSHION

FLAP

SPRINGS

3"

9"

2"

1/2" SUPPORTS

ELEVATION

5"

2 1/2"

REMOVABLE BACK CUSHION

HEXAGONAL
CUSHION
13" ON EACH SIDE

13"

45"

ARM SUPPORT

TOP VIEW

FRONT ELEVATION

FLAP

4"

13"

FLAP · DOUBLE
THICKNESS OF CARPET

60°

30°

BLUE TRIANGLES
SEAMS

TOP VIEW

1/2" REDWOOD
PLYWOOD - MITERED

HAIR FILLED CUSHION
COVERED WITH CARPET

6"

ELEVATION

1/2" REDWOOD PLYWOOD

OPEN

PLYWOOD SLAB OVER
SUPPORTS TO FASTEN
UPHOLSTERY

4"

12"

20"

1/2" REDWOOD PLYWOOD
SUPPORTS

5"

PLAN AT BASE

TOP VIEW

PLAN AT BASE

EASY CHAIR
MAKE 12 OF THESE

FLOOR CUSHION
MAKE 12 OF THESE

THE OTTOMAN
MAKE 12 OF THESE

Furniture details

Furnishing Our Home

Every house worth considering as a work of art must have a grammar of its own. "Grammar," in this sense, means the same thing in any construction—whether it be of words or of stone or wood. It is the shape-relationship between the various elements that enter into the constitution of the thing. The "grammar" of the house is its manifest articulation of all its parts. . . .

When the chosen grammar [of the building] is finally adopted . . . walls, ceilings, furniture, etc. become inspired by it. Everything has a related articulation in relation to the whole and all belongs together; looks well together because all together are speaking the same language.*

In selecting and placing furnishings for the Hanna House, we developed certain guidelines:

Our home was not to be a Sunday parlor or a cold museum, but a space to be lived in indoors and outdoors.

Our dwelling should accommodate harmonious and comfortable furniture; permit efficient housekeeping; accept, unobtrusively, textiles, sculpture, carvings, other *objets d'art,* books, and plants; it should unify indoors and outdoors and provide work stations that are quiet and restful to the senses.

We moved into an almost empty house in late autumn of 1937 and started to furnish it. As indicated earlier, very little furniture came with us from our rented house. With Mr. Wright's built-ins and these few odd pieces we managed to live for several months. Finally, the furniture maker in San Francisco completed our order, and we happily arranged and rearranged our two large, Wright-designed reading chairs, three hassocks, and three floor cushions. We had a splendid, heavy hexagonal redwood table made by our carpenters, which served as the children's playroom table and also as dining table for our family of five.

In 1947, while Paul was on duty in the Panama Canal Zone, he pur-

* Frank Lloyd Wright, The Natural House (New York, Horizon Press, 1954), p. 181.

chased a pile of discarded hardwood lying under a schoolhouse and shipped it to San Francisco via ocean freighter. When planed, the old planks proved to be beautiful Honduras mahogany, which we made into a banquet table in a hexagonal pattern, designed by Paul and approved by Mr. Wright. Finally we had a table of an appropriate size for our spacious dining room, the former playroom. With the addition or subtraction of table leaves, we could seat from six to thirty-six people. In Denmark we finally found the perfect dining chair. With Mr. Wright's approval, we acquired twenty-four teak chairs, with sea-rush or leather seats.

This may be a good point at which to say something about our response to Wright-designed furniture. We happen to like what Mr. Wright did for us. What did Mr. Wright think about his furniture? He was forever trying to get us to discard the two big Wright-designed chairs. On one occasion, visiting us, he said, "I have been in this business sixty years and I still can't design a piece of furniture. I don't understand my problem. I suppose I think too much in terms of a building and I wind up with that!"—poking with his cane the side of one of our reading chairs.

It is not true that Mr. Wright permitted only his own furniture in houses he designed. He admired the coffee table Paul designed and made from redwood burl. We brought back from the Orient a number of pieces of teak furniture, every one of which Mr. Wright approved.

After remodeling the main house in 1957, we asked Mr. Wright to design some low chairs for our living room, chairs suitable for short-legged people. We suggested that he modify a round chair he had designed for his son David's house, using the hexagon geometry rather than the circle. And he did. We think the handsome back, the shape of the seat, and the sloping arms all attractive. But chairs for short-legged people? Any six-foot-three, 250-pound guest would immediately choose one of the low chairs.

The library provides areas for reading, desk work, chatting, eating, or viewing the fireplace or the garden. Two Swan chairs from Denmark offer seating for viewing the garden and the pool cascade, or for reading. Two Danish "Egg" chairs together with the cushioned couch and a large Wright-designed reading chair form a semicircle for conversation by the fire or for viewing television. Tables can be set up for light meals by the fire.

Between the two working desks, attached to the ceiling, is a set of large roller-maps (we preferred to have them roll down from the ceiling rather than take up precious wall space). A sixteen-inch world globe with counter-weight is suspended over one desk.

Fireplace tools, designed by Mr. Wright, hang at the side of the library

(above) *A Wright-designed chair by the fireplace
the master bedroom, 1963
(below) View from dining room into laboratory, 1961
(right) View from living room into dining room, 1961*

fireplace. Against the east glass wall of the library is a bank of counters on which are the duplicator and an assortment of magazines. Below the counter tops are two-drawer filing cabinets, metal retracting mechanisms for the electric typewriter, calculator, transcriber, and other office equipment.

Throughout the house, most night lighting is provided by flood lamps in the decks or ceiling lights recessed in metal boxes behind Czechoslovakian glass. At locations where reading light must supplement deck or ceiling light, floor or table lamps are used. The house has over two hundred electrical outlets, switches, or other terminals, which make electrical current easily available everywhere.

In 1953 we replaced the linen Klearflax rugs with Woolturf carpeting. We followed Mr. Wright's original pattern, which allowed the hexagonal concrete tiles to show around the carpet perimeters in entry and living room. We chose color contrasts as in the original carpets, but used off-white and beige color contrasts. (This change pleased some of our Stanford alumni friends, who felt the original blue and gold—the colors of the University of California—somewhat disloyal.) Woolturf was very expensive but easier to maintain than the Klearflax and much more resistant to wear. The Woolturf was still in very good condition in 1976.

————————

The wealth of materials and art objects that beautify the impressive architecture of the two Wright homes (Taliesin and Taliesin West) encouraged us to adorn our home with objects acquired in our travels. Mr. Wright purposefully provided ideal spaces for present and future treasures. The decks (in every room) provided not only indirect lighting and visual aesthetic effects, but also space for display of collectibles. The fireplace hobs served either as extra seating or as bases for pieces of sculpture. The half-hexagonal alcoves provided nooks for chests, ceramic jars, or sculpture.

Mr. Wright himself enriched our house with products of his own creative hands: sculptures called *Nakoma* and *Nakomis,* Indian chief and squaw, replicas of a project for gate posts.

As a result of a mission to Yugoslavia, we became acquainted with the work of Yugoslavia's great sculptor, Ivan Mestrovic. The Mestrovics were both compatriots of Mrs. Wright and great admirers of Mr. Wright. The American Institute of Architects presented both Mr. Wright and Mr. Mestrovic with gold medals. Mrs. Mestrovic's affection for Mr. and Mrs. Wright and her admiration for our house persuaded her to allow us to have castings made of five of her husband's finest sculptures.* All of these sculp-

* *Moses, Odysseus, Prometheus Bound, Marco on Sarac, and Job.*

138

tures enhanced the beauty of the interior of the house.

As a young draftsman for Louis Sullivan, in Chicago, Mr. Wright was assigned the task of designing the ornament for the great proscenium arch of Sullivan's Garrick theater. When the theater was demolished, a friend of ours bought the entire arch and cut it into squares, each containing a sunburst medallion. We were fortunate recipients of several of these. We gave one to the art department at Stanford and one hangs, appropriately, on a wall in the Hanna House. Before the arrival of the medallion, the only painting hanging on the walls was a lovely watercolor of the house.*

Mr. Wright often talked to us about his experiences in Germany and the artists he met there. We did not forget this, and when we were in Germany (Paul serving with the Office of Military Government, U.S.) during the Occupation, we became acquainted with several painters and sculptors. Among these were Georg Kolbe and Hans Haffenrichter. Both men were great admirers of Mr. Wright and his architecture. Before we left Germany, both artists offered us castings of any pieces we chose. We selected *Adagio* and *Elegie* by Kolbe and *Eurydice* by Haffenrichter and gave the sculptures to the Stanford museum, with the understanding that we might borrow them for display in the Hanna House.

These treasures added to the hominess of the house and further enriched the architecture. They served as constant reminders of great experiences and gracious friends both here and abroad.

One is never finished with furniture and furnishings: some textiles fade, furniture does wear out, new technical advances produce better lighting, heating, plumbing, acoustics, or housekeeping conveniences. So the furnishings change. We know that furnishings and their arrangements will undergo changes in the future. We trust that no change will destroy the harmony and unity Mr. Wright fashioned for this home.

---

* *By Professor Daniel Mendelowitz, a colleague.*

View of the Hanna House from driveway

Outdoors

Organic architecture sees shelter not only as a quality of space but of spirit, and the prime factor in any concept of building man into his environment as a legitimate feature of it. Thus environment and building are one. Planting the grounds around the building on the site as well as adorning the building take on new importance as they become features harmonious with the space within-to-be-lived-in. Site, structure, furnishing-decoration too, plantings—all these become as one in organic architecture. . . .*

The outdoors was part of our home, part of our life, and we shaped our property accordingly. Important to our plan were the original trees on the hillside. There were white oaks that had grown from acorns probably buried decades earlier by ground squirrels. Mr. Wright had sited the buildings to preserve the oaks, and we gave them special care—pruning, feeding, and watering. The lone cypress, allowed to project through the roof of the carport, had a problem—bark beetles had worked on it for years. Mr. Wright encouraged us to nurse it along. We kept it alive and growing slowly by annually cutting the dead branches and spraying.

The trees provided shade in the summer and helped to frame the buildings. We installed electric lights in the oaks—some pointed upward to the branches and foliage and others turned downward, lighting the lawns and terraces. In the oak over the cascade, we concealed a floodlight in a birdhouse to enliven the water as it coursed from the upper to the lower pool. In the oak at the foot of the driveway we set small metal cylinders with low-wattage bulbs shining through star-shaped holes, creating a fairylike atmosphere for our guests as they drove up the hill for an evening party.

Pyracantha hedges were planted to break the site into lawn, orchard, and parking. Procumbent junipers and ivy served as ground cover to accentuate architectural features and to soften brick retaining walls. Brick flower boxes, using the hexagonal grammar of the house, were filled with

* Frank Lloyd Wright, A Testament (New York, Horizon Press, 1957), p. 227–228.

View of the shop from garden terrace

azaleas, camelias, and cymbidiums. Tubs on the terraces held rhododendrons, jade trees, rubber trees, bamboo, and lantana.

Mr. Wright suggested that we establish a line of tall conifers along the rear of the property, but we rejected this idea because we wished to look to the coastal range and particularly to Black Mountain. For the first decade in the house we also enjoyed watching cattle in the pasture. When colleagues built homes in this pasture on the hill behind us, we agreed to share the cost of a high wooden fence along the common boundary. On our side we planted a row of pyracantha bushes to soften the effect.*

With the Quillens, neighbors on the southwest, we planted flowering bushes, olive trees, and Arizona cypress trees as screens. With the Dodds, our neighbors on the northeast, we used the area between our houses as a common lawn set with fruit trees. We preferred trees, bushes, and vines that earned their keep by producing fruit. In the first decade of living at 737 Frenchman's Road, we enjoyed some kind of fresh fruit from our orchard every month of the year. There were over sixty varieties, including several apples, plums, cherries, and peaches. Some trees and bushes were exotic: jujubes, myrtus ugni, ice-cream sapotas, tangelos, and guavas. Other trees produced oranges, lemons, pears, apricots, prunes, loquats, figs, avocados, pomegranates, nectarines, and persimmons. Bushes and vines provided black and red currants, black and red raspberries, boysenberries, loganberries, gooseberries, and four varieties of grapes.

* We hope the university will some-day return to Mr. Wright's suggestion and plant the row of conifers along the south property line.

We learned the art of espaliering, applying it to figs, lemons, jujubes, and pyracanthas. In the lower orchard we constructed a hexagonal compost pit to accumulate grass clippings, raked leaves, and prunings. By watering and adding chemicals during the summer, we had cubic yards of humus to distribute over the orchard.

During World War II we maintained a Victory Garden below the front terrace. Due to the rich soil and chemical additives we had an abundance of fresh vegetables.

When we returned in 1952 from the Philippines, Jean suggested that we convert the Victory Garden into a driveway and parking area; "an inexpensive project," she said. Only three things needed to be done, she thought: 1) hire a tractor to cut and drag an oval driveway; 2) plant the center of the oval with grass and junipers; and 3) pave the driveway with apricot pits obtained free from the local canneries.

We built our driveway and parking area, but before we finished Mr. Wright designed a long brick retaining wall and steps from the front terrace down to the parking area. We paved the new driveway with rock and asphalt, put in a lawn sprinkler system, planted a rose hedge and junipers, transplanted an orange and a lemon tree, and installed ground flood lights for night parking. Not inexpensive! But a satisfying solution that pleased both the Hannas and Mr. Wright.

We admired the artifacts that graced Mr. Wright's gardens and consequently brought from abroad many art objects that we thought would fit our landscape. For instance, in the garden of our house stands a two-ton Oya-lava stone urn designed by Mr. Wright for the Imperial Hotel in Tokyo. Paul was staying at the Imperial when the wreckers commenced its demolition. Paul asked our owner friends, the Inumarus, if we might have one of the sculptured pieces from the hotel to take home to Stanford. Mr. Inumaru graciously gave us one of the urns from the porte-cochere, saying that it was appropriate for Mr. Wright's sculptured urn from the Imperial to rest in the garden of Mr. Wright's Stanford house. It cost us a small fortune to get the heavy piece down from high on the façade, wrapped, crated, and shipped to San Francisco. Stanford trucked the urn to the Hanna House, where a crane lifted it onto a concrete foundation Paul had prepared.

We were unsuccessful in maintaining grass under the great oak south of the main house, so Paul designed a paving of cement and river rock to replace the grass. Exploring the creek beds of our tree farm, he returned with two large tree-root systems. He bored a half-inch hole through one stump, drove a pipe through it, connected the pipe to the water system, and fixed

143

The back garden

North terrace

the inverted stump in the center of the space. With the water turned on, a fine spray from a sprinkler head moistens and preserves the stump, and brings out the natural colors of the wood. This was so pleasing that we prepared the second stump and placed it at the top of the cascade.

Our entrance driveway up a steep hill was terrifying to timid drivers, so we planted floribunda rose bushes along the outer edge. When these matured, drivers were not conscious that the hill dropped off precipitously. After forty years these bushes still are blooming profusely. Below the floribunda hedge we planted Arizona cypress, pyracantha bushes, and whatever would hold the soil on the steep bank. We scattered wildflower seeds to add a touch of color.

In the brick flower boxes on the east terrace we planted cymbidium bulbs from which thirty blossoming orchid spikes delighted us each spring. Along the brick wall on the east terrace, we brightened the area with pansies and daffodils. Part of the south lawn became a small rose garden. The flower boxes on north and south exposures were filled with azaleas and camelias. The garage trellis was draped with honeysuckle. Along the carport driveway, chrysanthemums flourished. Our Basque gardener lavished loving care on the garden and added a professional touch we lacked.

Our first venture in satisfying a desire to see and hear running water was the transformation of a brick flower box off the living room terrace into a small fish pool. Paul fashioned drip dishes out of three old plowshare disks, in the style of Taliesin. The sound of the water splashing from disk to disk and into the pool pleased us and attracted families of small song thrushes, who came to bathe, sing, and drink.

Mr. Wright was no longer living in 1960 when we were ready to build the summerhouse, pools, and cascade. Consequently William Wesley Peters, the senior member of the Taliesin Associated Architects, refined the original 1936 plan.

With the completion of the garden of the Hanna House, we felt we might rest for a while from building activity; the main architectural tasks were now accomplished. Only the conversion of the shop into a caretaker's apartment remained to be done. Mr. Wright could never see the finished garden setting for our home, but we could picture him sitting on the terrace, enjoying the play of light and shadow and listening to a symphony of wind chimes, cascade, and song birds. We know Mr. Wright would have been satisfied that Hanna House is in reality far more gratifying to us than anything we had ever anticipated.

View from garden house

Garden house and terrace

BIBLIOGRAPHIC NOTE

In his *Frank Lloyd Wright: An Annotated Bibliography* (Los Angeles: Hennessey & Ingalls, Inc., 1978), Robert L. Sweeney provides the most complete Frank Lloyd Wright bibliography available at this time. There are, however, several titles specifically related to the Hanna House that do not appear in Mr. Sweeney's book and some that were published after it appeared:

Carie, Maison, *et. al.* "Space Organization of Housing and Images of Living through the Study of the P. Hanna House." In Japanese. *The Kenchiku Bunka* 21 (April, 1966).

Editors of *AIA Journal.* "Hexagonal-Module Wright House Is Placed on National Register." *AIA Journal* 68 (May, 1979).

Feldman, Edmund Burke. *Art as Image and Idea.* Englewood Cliffs, NJ: Prentice-Hall, 1967.

Gutheim, Frederick. "The Turning Point in Mr. Wright's Career." *AIA Journal* 69 (June, 1980).

Hanks, David A. *The Decorative Designs of Frank Lloyd Wright.* New York: E.P. Dutton, 1979.

————. *The Decorative Designs of Frank Lloyd Wright.* Washington, D.C.: Superintendent of Documents, U.S. Printing Office, 1977.

Moore, Charles W. "Because We Aren't Going to Keep It Unless It Works." *Perspecta.* New Haven, CT: The Yale University Architectural Journal, 1967.

Storrer, William Allin. "New Zealand's Architectural Generation Gap." *New Zealand Institute of Architects* 61 (October, 1974).

Wright, Frank Lloyd. "Frank Lloyd Wright." *Architectural Forum* 68 (January, 1938).

————. *Selected Drawings Portfolio.* [2nd portfolio] New York: Horizon Press, 1979.

For further reading about Frank Lloyd Wright in general, we would like to suggest:

Jacobs, Herbert and Catherine. *Building With Frank Lloyd Wright.* San Francisco: Chronicle Books, 1979.

Insolera, Italo. "Wright in Italia; 1921–1963." *Comunità.* Milan: Comunità (April, 1964).

Spencer, Brian A., ed. *The Prairie School Tradition.* New York: Whitney Library of Design, 1979.

Tafel, Edgar. *Apprentice to Genius.* New York: McGraw-Hill, 1979.

PHOTOGRAPHIC SOURCES

All numbers refer to page numbers.

The letters, notes, drawings, and telegrams by Frank Lloyd Wright and letters from the office of Frank Lloyd Wright are copyright © 1981 Frank Lloyd Wright Foundation.

Air-Photo Company, Inc.: 120
John Amarantides (courtesy of The Frank Lloyd Wright Memorial Foundation): 122, 145 (top)
The Architectural Forum: 80
Morley Baer: 88, 99, 116 (top and bottom), 118, 119, 137 (bottom left), 142, 145 (bottom)
Esther Born, photographer: 79 (top and bottom), 83 (top and bottom), 84, 85, 86 (bottom), 87, 89
The Frank Lloyd Wright Memorial Foundation: 12, 26, 38
Leo Holub: 140
Richard Keeble: 22
Stanford University News and Publications Service: 127 (top and bottom)
George Stefan: 69, 71, 73, 100, 134
Ezra Stoller (ESTO): 9, 10, 11, 101-108, 137 (top left, right), 143 (top and bottom)
Sunset Magazine: 14, 98, 120
Madeline Thatcher (courtesy of *House Beautiful*): 110, 115, 117
Chris Mari van Dyck: 62 (top and bottom), 86 (top), 110

The color illustration of the presentation drawing has been supplied by The Frank Lloyd Wright Memorial Foundation. All other color photographs were supplied by Ezra Stoller (© ESTO), to whom we give grateful thanks.
All other photographs were taken by the authors.